What People Are Saying

"Embracing Retirement" is a refreshing and deeply compassionate guide for anyone navigating life after work. With warmth, honesty, and lived experience, Gary Fretwell invites readers to explore retirement not as an ending, but as a powerful new beginning. His thoughtful reflections and gentle challenges help retirees rediscover their purpose, reshape their days with intention, and reconnect with their deeper selves.

What makes this book stand out is its focus on the emotional journey—addressing the often-unspoken feelings of loss, restlessness, and identity shifts with grace and clarity. It offers more than advice; it offers companionship. For any senior seeking meaning, connection, and joy in this next chapter.

Kathy McFadden, CEO
Prescott Adult Center

Gary Fretwell offers a practical toolbox of ideas for those retired, nearing retirement, or restless in it. Inside are examples, thought-provoking questions, and exercises to support a fulfilling transition. Drawing on a 25-year planning career and personal reflection, he encourages readers to treat the book as a ready-to-use workbook for embracing retirement with intention.

Robert Painter - Philanthropist, Non-Profit Leader, Community Leader

Embracing Retirement is a wonderful word map filled with smart simple strategies for a joyful, purposeful, and powerful retirement. These versatile strategies can make retirement the relaxed productive time it could be, no should be. Whether you are newly retired, or have been for many years, this book is a perfect read for individuals who want to incorporate meaning into their retirement years.

A very uplifting read.

Jeri Henderson- Enthusiastic Volunteer for Prescott Meals on Wheels and Happily Retired Bank Officer

I loved this soon to be published book! Have some friends that could help them too.

After reading Embracing retirement, it opened my eyes with enthusiasm and not feeling fearful. Great and to the point questions were brought up, issues and things that I had never thought about. I feel less anxious about diving into retirement. This book gave me ideas about how filling a new purpose in my next chapter in my life can be. Still feeling happy and truly understanding what really matters to me.

Clara Nakata - Nurse, Approaching retirement

Embracing Retirement:
Discovering Your Fulfilling Second Act

Gary L. Fretwell
#1 International Best-Selling Author

Embracing Retirement:

Discovering Your Fulfilling Second Act

Copyright @ 2025 by Gary L. Fretwell

Fretwell Solutions

https://garyfretwell.com

All rights reserved. No part of this publication may be reproduced distributed or transmitted in any form or by any means including photocopying recording or other electronic or mechanical means without proper written permission of author, except in the case of brief quotations embodied in critical reviews and certain other noncommercial uses permitted by copyright law.

ISBN 979-8-9919467-5-9 (paperback)

ISBN 979-8-9919467-4-2 (eBook)

Visit us online at https://garyfretwell.com

Printed in United States of America

About the Cover Art

Created by Nancy Fretwell, the cover art beautifully mirrors the journey of retirement.

A single line begins—sharp, imperfect, and uncertain—much like the early moments of this life transition. It meanders, bends, and shifts course, reflecting the unpredictability of what's next.

But as it moves forward, it gains confidence and space—symbolizing how retirement can unfold into something clear, peaceful, and deeply fulfilling.

Visual Metaphor:

- The thin, fractured line on the left suggests vulnerability and the end of a chapter.
- As the line sweeps forward, it becomes more fluid and expansive.
- Its curved, imperfect path reflects the grace in change and the beauty of forging a new direction.
- It ultimately dissolves into openness—representing clarity, freedom, and possibility.

This artwork reminds us: retirement isn't an ending. It's a soft, elegant beginning.

Dedication

Uncle Carl has been more than family—he's been a mentor, a role model, and a steady presence through every season of my life. He taught me the value of hard work, the importance of character, and now, the grace of embracing retirement. His wisdom and quiet strength have shaped who I am. Thank you, Uncle Carl, for being a rock in my life.

To my brothers: When we were young, we stuck together because we had to—because life gave us no other choice. We faced a lot with very little, and we got through it side by side. Later in life, we've stayed close not out of necessity, but out of love and choice.

Randy, who we lost this past year, is deeply missed. His passing left a space that can never be filled. I miss you brother!

Phil—my youngest brother—you've always had a personality that fills the room. You carry a boundless energy and an unstoppable spirit that reminds me so much of Dad. Like him, you've never met a stranger, and people are drawn to your warmth, humor, and heart. You've lived boldly, loved deeply, and somehow managed to do it all with grace and grit. Through every twist and turn in my life, you've been there—not just as a brother, but as a steady presence I could always count on. I don't say it enough, but I'm deeply grateful for the relationship we have. I love you brother.

This book was written with the love, encouragement, and inspiration of these three incredible men. I wouldn't be the same without them.

Acknowledgments

Writing this book has been both a professional journey and a deeply personal one—and I could not have done it alone.

First, I want to thank the many individuals who have mentored me throughout my life. You challenged me to think more deeply, live more intentionally, and serve more generously. Your wisdom helped shape not only my career but the way I approach this new chapter of life.

To my family—thank you for your unconditional love and support. You have been my foundation, my cheering section, and my compass. To my wife, whose encouragement, patience, and belief in me made this book possible: your partnership is my greatest gift.

I'm especially grateful to the countless individuals I've had the privilege to speak with over the years about retirement. Your stories, questions, concerns, and insights have informed every page of this book. You reminded me that retirement is not an end but a new beginning—full of possibility, purpose, and personal growth.

This book is for all of you. Thank you for helping me embrace this journey—and for inspiring others to do the same.

Table of Contents

Introduction	1
Chapter 1: The Question That Changes Everything	9
Chapter 2: Designing Your Days with Intention.	18
Chapter 3: Reconnecting with Purpose.	31
Chapter 4: The Power of Contribution.	54
Chapter 5: The Emotional Undercurrents.	76
Chapter 6: Relationships in Transition.	103
Chapter 7: Staying Sharp—Mind, Body, and Spirit.	132
Chapter 8: Planning for the Unexpected.	149
Chapter 9: Reimagining Work in Retirement.	172
Chapter 10: Creativity in the Second Act.	192
Chapter 11: A Retirement Built on Gratitude.	212
Chapter 12: Living Your Legacy.	233
Conclusion: Living Forward with Intention	249
Embracing Retirement Workbook.	255
About the Author	274

Introduction

"Embracing Retirement: Discovering Your Fulfilling Second Act"

I recently had a conversation with my uncle as always, he had some wisdom to impart to me. We were talking about me being on 2 board and president of both. How I had launched my business, Fretwell Solutions that included writing books, consulting, speaking and coaching. I also excitedly shared with him I had just launched a new website: garyfretwell.com.

After listening to me go on and on. He came out with a statement that spurred me to write this book. He said Gary, "You know what, you suck at retirement!"

Wow thanks Uncle Carl probably true.

As I thought about it, I wondered if I really did suck at it. So, I thought I would start doing some research and learn how to retire. After all, I didn't have a game plan, I pretty much just kept up the pace I have had for the last 40 years. Seemed normal to me.

So, the book you have in your hand is me writing down my thoughts and findings as I got into it. As I reflect on my own "retirement" journey through these uncharted times, I found myself thinking, I've done pretty good at it, but I can sure improve on a bunch. At 71, I've felt a mix of excitement and nervousness, like a rollercoaster that never stops. It's a time when many of our dreams of adventure and new starts, but it's also a time when we can't help but wonder what the future holds. During this stage of life, I think many of us say, what's next?

When I first stepped away from my daily routine—a routine that had been a significant part of my identity for over four decades—I was faced with questions that many of us grapple with:

What does this new chapter truly mean? Will I find the fulfillment I seek, or will I drift aimlessly through a sea of leisure and boredom.

What I've come to grips with, through my experiences and conversations with others, is that retirement can be one of the most enriching and joyful times of our lives.

We are living in an era that that is redefining what it means to retire. No longer is it a time to just sit around watching tv or playing endless rounds of golf; it is an invitation to seek out new adventures and interests. It's our chance to rediscover who we are outside the confines of our prior work life. We can explore passions that may have had for years but have been stuck away in our minds. This is a chance to learn that language I've always wanted to learn, to learn new skills, like painting or playing the guitar. Also, maybe for the first time in my life I have time to forge connections that bring joy and a sense of meaning to my life.

Yet, let's not sugarcoat it. Navigating these new experiences can be a challenging. As we age, our bodies and minds require more attention and care, I've discovered this the hard way at times. We face the reality of physical changes, health issues, and the emotional challenges with realizing we are simply human, and these changes are a part of life.

Hopefully, all these changes, convince us of the importance of health and wellness. Throughout my own experience, I have learned the profound impact that prioritizing my physical and mental well-being can have on our overall quality of my life. Many of these changes are in sharp contrast to my life before retirement where I thought self-care was nice, but who had time for it. Simple changes in behavior—such as taking regular walks in nature, maintaining a balanced diet, and incorporating moments of mindfulness into my daily routines has significantly improved my energy levels, enhanced my mood, and created a sense of vitality that allows me to fully engage in the activities we love. Some of the things you will find in this book will do the same for you.

In "Embracing Retirement: Discovering Your Fulfilling Second Act," my desire is to share not only practical strategies but also the warmth and wisdom that comes from the shared experiences of those who have walked this path before us. Together, we will explore a myriad of ways to make this second act not just bearable but joyful. We will delve into the art of discovering new hobbies that ignite our passions, engaging in lifelong learning that keeps our minds sharp, and building meaningful relationships that foster a sense of community and support.

We will discuss the importance of setting goals—short-term and long-term—that align with your unique dreams and aspirations. Whether it's volunteering for a cause close to your heart, traveling to places you've always wanted to visit, or simply spending quality time with family and friends, each choice we make can contribute to a richer, more fulfilling retirement experience.

During the reading this book, I hope you learn how to grapple with the emotional landscape of retirement, address feelings of loss, shifts in your identity from being what your profession and title were. In addition, perhaps this is a chance to reinvent yourself. Yes, it's never too late to do that, why not now. In fact, this is an important point. For most of us, our day-to-day obligations and demands are significantly reduced. Why not take this new freedom, go do and be who you have always wanted to be. I believe that sharing stories—both our struggles and triumphs—can empower us to embrace this change with a sense of grace and passion.

Each of us has a unique story to tell, and by weaving these stories together, we can create a tapestry of inspiration and encouragement that will light the way for ourselves and others.

So, let's embark on this journey together. Each day presents us with an opportunity to paint a new picture of what our retirement can look like. It's time to embrace the adventure ahead, to fill our days with purpose, laughter, and the simple joys that make life truly fulfilling.

I invite you to join me as we explore how to make the most of this extraordinary time—a time that can be as rich and rewarding as anything we've experienced before. Together, let's unlock the potential of our "retirement "years. Let's create a life that reflects our true selves, one filled with love, exploration, and a lot of fun along the way.

Chapter 1

The Question That Changes Everything

Let me start with a question—one I've asked hundreds of people over the past seven years. It's a question that rarely gets a quick answer and often sparks something deeper than expected:

"What do you want your retirement to feel like?"

Not look like.

Not sound like.

Not a bucket list of exotic destinations or a week-by-week breakdown of activities.

I'm asking about the emotional experience of retirement.

What do you want to feel when you wake up each morning in this new chapter of life?

Peace? Joy? Excitement? Contribution? Freedom? Belonging?

When I pose this question in workshops or one-on-one conversations, there's usually a pause. People blink, lean back, and say something like, "Huh... I've never really thought about it like that."

They've thought about the numbers—believe me, they've all thought about the numbers.

They know their retirement date, their investment strategy, their healthcare plan.

They've dreamed of more travel, more time with family, more rest.

But when I ask how they want retirement to feel—they pause.

And in that pause lies the door to a far more meaningful conversation.

Not the End, but a Turning Point

Retirement is often framed as an ending. You've crossed the finish line. You've paid your dues, and now you can rest.

But I'd like to offer a different metaphor: retirement is not the end of the road—it's a scenic detour with fewer road signs and more open space to explore.

It's a profound shift. One where external expectations fade, and internal questions rise to the surface.

- Who am I now that I'm no longer the boss, the caretaker, the go-to person?

- What matters to me now?

- Where will I find my sense of purpose without a title or a deadline?

These aren't easy questions. But they are essential questions.

Because if we don't ask them, we risk drifting into a version of retirement that's technically restful—but emotionally flat. And that's not what you've worked for.

What I've learned in my own journey—and in guiding others through theirs—is this: retirement can be one of the richest, most creative, most personally rewarding stages of life. But only if we approach it with the same thoughtfulness and courage we applied to our careers.

What No One Tells You About Retirement

Retirement brochures will show you happy couples on sailboats or sandy beaches. But real life? It's more nuanced.

Here's what I hear from many people after the initial "honeymoon" phase of retirement fades:

• "I thought I'd feel free, but I actually feel a little lost."

• "I'm not sure where I'm needed anymore."

• "My schedule is wide open, but my motivation is low."

• "The pace of life changed… but I haven't caught up emotionally."

These aren't complaints. They're insights.

They point to a deeper hunger—one that financial planning alone can't satisfy.

What we're really seeking is purpose. Connection. Growth. Relevance.

We want to feel that our presence still matters. That we're still becoming.

Retirement isn't just about doing less. It's about choosing differently.

Choosing how to invest your energy, your wisdom, your compassion.

Choosing to be a student again. A mentor. A guide. A curious soul with time to explore what really lights you up.

A New Kind of Question

So let me offer you a new kind of retirement question. One that doesn't focus on logistics, but on identity:

"Who do I want to become in this next chapter?"

It's a question that has no wrong answer—only honest ones. And it invites a kind of self-discovery that's incredibly life-giving.

- Do you want to be more curious?

- More present with the people you love.

- More generous with your time and wisdom?

- Do you want to create something? Reconnect with something? Heal something?

- Do you want to laugh more? Reflect more? Be bolder?

The beauty of this question is that it reminds you that you're not done. You're still evolving. You still get to shape the story.

Retirement is not a period at the end of the sentence. It's a comma. A pause. And then a brand-new paragraph you get to write.

A Moment of Truth

If you're willing, I'd like to invite you into a simple practice.

Set aside ten minutes. No distractions—just you, your thoughts, and a quiet space.

Grab a notebook or open a blank document. And gently ask yourself:

"What do I want to feel more of in this season of life?"

Don't chase the perfect answer. Just write what comes. Words, phrases, even emotions. Let your inner wisdom speak.

Maybe your list includes words like:

- Peace

- Contribution

- Wonder

- Playfulness

- Depth

- Joy

- Stillness

Whatever shows up on your page—trust it.

That's your compass.

It doesn't mean you need to overhaul your life tomorrow. It simply means you're beginning to pay attention—to listen more deeply to your soul's desires.

And that, my friend, is how this journey begins.

An Invitation to Thrive

This book is your companion in that journey. It's not a manual. It's not a checklist.

It's a series of reflections, questions, and stories to guide you gently back to yourself—back to the truest version of who you are and who you're becoming.

As someone who's walked this road—and continues to—I can tell you this:

Retirement is not about stepping away from relevance.

It's about stepping into a life that's more authentically yours than ever before.

Let's walk this together. Let's not just retire—

Let's reawaken. Let's reimagine. Let's live forward.

Because your second act?

It might just be your most meaningful one yet.

Chapter 2

Designing Your Days with Intention

It's a quiet Tuesday morning.

No rush. No emails waiting. No meetings cluttering the calendar. The coffee's warm, your golden retriever is snoring gently by the back door, and for a moment—you pause.

And you ask yourself:

"So… now what?"

Welcome to retirement.

This isn't the question they asked at those retirement seminars. It's not about your portfolio or your Medicare options. No one warned you that the biggest challenge of retirement might not be financial—it might be existential.

Because now, for the first time in maybe decades, you're staring at an open calendar. And with it, the rarest thing in modern life: freedom.

That freedom? It's both a gift—and a challenge.

The Trap of Unstructured Time

At first, the idea of unstructured time sounds like a long-awaited reward. You wake up when you want. No one's asking for reports, scheduling back-to-back Zoom meetings, or expecting a quick reply to an urgent email. There's a deep exhale that comes with that freedom—one that feels earned after years of hustle, sacrifice, and tight schedules.

But here's what most people don't tell you: unstructured time, when left unchecked, slowly starts to drain your sense of purpose.

In the beginning, it's pleasant—delightful, even. You sleep in a little. Enjoy a leisurely breakfast. Run a few errands. Take a walk. Watch a movie in the middle of the afternoon just because you can. There's no guilt. Just a quiet kind of joy.

But then… a shift begins.

You find yourself staying up later and waking up later. You might open your calendar and see a full day of blank space, and instead of feeling excited, you feel uncertain. You start to drift—not in a peaceful way, but in a way that feels a little disconnected. A little off. Days blur into each other. You catch yourself asking, "Wait, what day is it again?"

What was once freedom starts to feel more like fog.

You've likely lived decades where time wasn't yours—it belonged to your profession, your clients, your kids, your community. You had roles, responsibilities, deadlines. You were accountable to something bigger than yourself. And even if you were overworked at times, you knew where you were needed.

Now, without those external demands, you're left with a wide-open space—and that space can feel disorienting. Because when your time no longer shapes you, it can start to unmoor you.

This isn't about productivity for productivity's sake. It's about identity.

You may not realize how much your identity was tied to your structured days until that structure is gone. For many, it's the first time in years—maybe ever—that no one else is setting the agenda. And for some, that can feel less like liberation and more like… being lost.

This is why some retirees experience what I call "purpose withdrawal."

Not because they don't care. But because they haven't yet learned how to reclaim their time with intention.

Here's the truth: Time doesn't stay neutral. If you don't direct it, it'll fill itself—usually with distractions, default habits, or vague feelings of guilt that you should be doing more.

And so, one of the most empowering steps you can take is to flip the script.

Instead of seeing unstructured time as a void to be filled, start seeing it as a canvas to be painted. You are no longer at the mercy of the clock—you are its designer. And that mindset shift? It's where the second act truly begins.

From Calendar Slave to Life Architect

For most of our lives, the calendar has been our boss.

It told us when to get up, when to go, where to be, and what to do. It was filled with color-coded appointments, back-to-back meetings, to-do lists, and responsibilities. Every block of time had a name, a task, or a deadline attached to it. There was a kind of security in that—even if it was exhausting.

And now?

Now that structure is gone. The calendar is blank. And that blankness can be surprisingly intimidating.

In retirement, you move from being a calendar slave to having an entirely new role—the architect of your life. And that's a powerful transition… if you choose to own it.

But let's be honest—it's tempting to let the days just flow. After all, you've earned the right to relax, to slow down. And you absolutely should. But if we're not careful, "relaxation" can slowly morph into passivity. We start to float instead of steer.

And here's where the risk comes in: if you don't design your time with intention, it will default to whatever grabs your attention. And in today's world, that usually means screens, shallow routines, and the numbing hum of "just staying busy."

You see, blank space on a calendar isn't just time—it's potential. And potential, when left untapped, can become regret.

So, how do you shift from default to design?

You start by remembering this: your time is now a mirror. It reflects to you what you truly value.

And if your calendar is a blank canvas, what do you want your life to look like when it's painted?

Ask yourself:

- What gives me energy?

- When do I feel most alive?

- Who do I want to spend more time with?

- What have I always said I'd do "someday"?

Then begin to carve out intentional blocks of time that reflect those answers.

Not every hour needs a label. You're not trying to recreate the rigid schedule of your working life. This is about anchoring your days with purpose—giving shape to the hours that matter most.

Imagine this:

- Mornings for solitude—maybe with a book, a cup of coffee, or a walk.

- Late mornings for contribution—mentoring someone, volunteering, or engaging with your community.

- Afternoons for creativity—writing, painting, learning, or building something with your hands.

- Evenings for connection and rest—a good meal, time with loved ones, or quiet reflection.

These aren't obligations. They're opportunities.

You're not being driven by deadlines—you're being drawn by meaning.

I've come to believe that retirement isn't an end—it's a new kind of beginning. One that gives you full creative control over how your time, and your life, unfolds.

And when you embrace that role—as the architect of your own days—you start to realize something remarkable: you don't need to be told what to do to have a meaningful day.

You already know. You just need to listen, choose, and begin.

The Power of a Simple Rhythm

When I first stepped into a slower season of life—no daily deadlines, no boardroom meetings, no packed calendar—I expected to feel instant peace. But instead, I felt... disoriented.

For years, my life had been dictated by rhythms I didn't create. The workday, the school calendar, the weekly commitments. Then one day, it all just... stopped. And in that stillness, I realized something important: without rhythm, my days began to lose their shape—and so did I.

So, I made one small, but transformative choice:

I gave my mornings a purpose.

Not a checklist. Not a rigid routine. But a gentle rhythm—one that honored what my body, mind, and spirit needed. One that anchored me.

Here's what that rhythm looked like for me:

- First hour: I read. Something meaningful. Maybe it was a few pages of a spiritual reflection, a biography, or a book that stirred my thinking and stretched my heart. This wasn't about speed-reading or checking a box. It was about nourishment.

- Second hour: I wrote. Sometimes journaling, sometimes sketching out ideas, sometimes just letting thoughts find their way onto the page. Writing helped me process the quiet. It helped me listen to what I was feeling, not just what I was doing.

- Third hour: I moved. I didn't hit the gym or train for a marathon. I walked the dog. I stretched. I breathed. I looked at the sky. I let my body catch up with my spirit.

At first, it didn't seem like much. But over time, those three simple anchors became the framework for how I wanted to live—not just in the morning, but throughout the day.

This rhythm wasn't about productivity. It was about presence.

And slowly, almost without realizing it, I began to feel more like myself again.

More grounded. More centered. More alive.

Because here's the truth I had to relearn we don't need to do more to feel fulfilled—we need to feel more aligned. When your mornings start with intention, the rest of the day tends to follow.

Try This Today: Your Ideal Morning

You don't need a perfect plan. You don't need an app or a timer or a resolution.

You just need to ask yourself one simple question:

If I could design the first 90 minutes of my day to nourish my mind, body, and spirit—what would I include?

Really think about it. Picture it. Feel it.

Would it be:

- A slow cup of coffee by the window before the world wakes up.

- Ten minutes of stretching or movement to reconnect with your body?

- A devotional or reflection that centers your thoughts.

- A walk with your dog—or just with your thoughts?

- Time to write, draw, pray, or breathe?

Write down three things. Nothing fancy. Nothing overwhelming. Just you, starting your day in a way that reflects who you are—and who you're becoming.

And tomorrow morning? Try it.

No pressure. No perfection. Just presence.

Then notice how the rest of the day feels. Notice the difference in your energy, your mindset, your heart.

Because when you design your morning with care, you begin to reshape your day with purpose.

And when you reshape your day, you begin to reshape your life—one quiet moment at a time.

Coming Up: Reconnecting with Purpose

So, what's next?

Because while designing your day is powerful, there's an even deeper question waiting beneath it all:

What's calling you now? What lights you up? What feels meaningful—not just for today, but for this whole season of life?

In the next chapter, we'll go there. We'll talk about purpose—the kind that doesn't end with your career but might just be waiting for you in this next act.

Let's take that next step together.

Purpose isn't behind you. It's waiting in your next choice.

Let's go find it together.

Chapter 3

Reconnecting with Purpose

Let's talk about something that most retirement conversations politely sidestep—purpose.

Not the surface-level kind. Not "stay busy" or "keep your mind sharp." I'm talking about the deeper, soul-stirring kind of purpose. The why-am-I-here question that lingers once the job titles are gone and the calendar opens wide. The kind of purpose that gives your day shape and your spirit direction.

Here's a truth I've learned the hard way—and through hundreds of conversations:

When we walk away from a job, a title, or a long-held role, we don't just hand in a badge or close a laptop.

We often hand over our sense of being needed.

And that absence can echo.

More Than Just Staying Active

I can't tell you how many conversations I've had that go like this:

"So, how's retirement treating you?"
"Oh, I'm keeping busy!"

There's often a quick smile with that response, maybe even a touch of pride. It sounds good. It sounds productive. And for a while, it feels like the right answer. After all, none of us want to admit we feel bored, unmoored, or unsure of what comes next.

But let's press pause for a moment and ask: What does "keeping busy" really mean?

Because in my experience, busyness is often a stand-in for something we haven't yet figured out how to name.

It's a safe place. A socially acceptable answer. A distraction from the deeper truth that maybe, just maybe, we feel a little disoriented—especially after a life spent in motion, surrounded by structure, deadlines, and expectations.

Busy is easy.

You can fill your time with errands, appointments, TV shows, house projects, clubs, even endless volunteering. But here's the thing—you can be busy and still feel like something's missing.

You can have a full calendar and still feel a little empty inside.

And that feeling? It's not a failure. It's a clue.

It's your heart's way of saying, "There's more."

More than just movement. More than filling time. More than staying active for the sake of activity.

Because here's the truth: activity and purpose are not the same thing.

- Activity keeps you moving.

- Purpose keeps you aligned.

Activity gives you a schedule.

Purpose gives you direction.

Activity can keep the days full.

Purpose makes the days feel meaningful.

This doesn't mean that staying active is wrong—far from it. Physical activity, social engagement, intellectual stimulation… they're all valuable parts of a healthy life.

But if all your movement lacks intention, it begins to feel like noise. Like you're turning up the volume on your life, hoping it drowns out the silence of uncertainty.

What you're really looking for is something that gives your time meaning.

Something that, when the day is done, leaves you feeling not just tired, but satisfied.

Not just entertained but enriched.

Not just busy—but alive.

Sometimes, that starts with a shift in how you approach even the most ordinary activities. A morning walk becomes a time of reflection. A phone call to a friend becomes a lifeline of connection. Baking cookies for a neighbor becomes an act of kindness that ripples outward.

It's not what you do—it's the why behind it that begins to matter more and more.

The next time someone asks, "How's retirement?"

Pause for a beat. Ask yourself—not just what you're doing, but how it feels.

And if your honest answer is, "I'm busy, but I'm not fulfilled," that's not a problem. That's an invitation.

An invitation to move from motion to meaning.

From activity to alignment.

From busyness to purpose.

Because you weren't made just to stay active. You were made to live deeply, love fully, and give meaningfully—even, and especially, in this next chapter of life.

You Had Purpose—Now You Get to Redefine It

If you built a career, raised a family, ran a business, led a team, mentored young people, or served your community—then yes, you absolutely had purpose. You were anchored in it, even if you didn't always call it that.

You showed up every day because others were counting on you. Because deadlines loomed. Because children needed rides, clients needed guidance, students needed leadership, or staff needed direction. Your value was often tied to how well you could meet the expectations of others. And you met them—time and time again.

But here's something we don't talk about enough:

Purpose born from responsibility is different than purpose born from choice.

Responsibility says, "I'm needed, so I'll step up."

Choice says, "I'm drawn to this—it lights me up, it brings me joy, it feels right."

That's the shift retirement invites us to make.

For the first time in a long time, no one is handing you a script.

There are no annual reviews. No grades. No promotions or gold stars.

It's just you—and your freedom.

And while that freedom can feel exhilarating, it can also be a little unnerving. When we're no longer defined by external roles, we must ask a far more personal question:

Who am I now that no one is telling me who to be?

That's a question of identity. Of alignment. Of rediscovery. And the answer doesn't come from outside—it comes from within.

So, take a deep breath and give yourself permission to explore:

- What matters to me now?

- What do I want to give my energy to—not because I should, but because I choose to?

- What feels meaningful, even if no one sees it or praises it?

This new kind of purpose isn't about productivity for productivity's sake.

It's not about staying busy to avoid boredom. It's about choosing meaning over motion.

It's about giving yourself fully to the things that matter deeply to you—whether that's nurturing your creativity, deepening your relationships, serving in your community, or simply being more present to the moments that used to pass you by.

The Power of Choosing Purpose

Here's what I've found:

The shift from "I have to" to "I get to" is one of the most liberating—and powerful—transformations a person can make in this next season.

- You had to lead that team.

- You had to make those decisions.

- You had to get the kids to school, manage the budget, run the meetings.

Now?

- You get to be intentional with your time.

- You get to invest in people and passions that align with your heart.

- You get to design a life around meaning instead of metrics.

This is your chance to build a purpose that nourishes you, not one that drains you. A purpose that you choose each morning—not because someone's depending on you, but because it reflects who you've become.

And maybe, just maybe, this purpose feels less like duty and more like joy.

Maybe it's quiet and personal. Maybe it's public and impactful. But most importantly, it's yours.

So go ahead and redefine it.

You've earned the right to ask, not "What do others need from me?" but instead:

What brings me fully to life?
What legacy do I want to live, not just leave?
Where do I want to show up—not out of obligation, but out of love?

This isn't starting over. It's starting true.

And that kind of purpose? That's the kind that will carry you—not just through retirement, but into a life of deep, sustained meaning.

A Story: The Retired Dean and the Garden

Let me tell you about someone I worked with a few years ago—a retired university dean.

Brilliant man. Deep thinker. Spent 35 years leading departments, shaping futures, making decisions that mattered. But when he retired, he confessed something quietly: "I don't feel needed anymore."

He said, "I used to get a hundred emails a day. Now, nothing. I'm not on anyone's radar."

I asked him gently, "Who says you're not needed?"

After some hesitation and some brainstorming, he agreed to help a neighbor at a community garden. At first, it felt beneath him—pulling weeds, watering vegetables. He joked that the tomatoes weren't asking him for strategic plans.

But something started to shift. As he showed up consistently, he began mentoring younger volunteers. He shared leadership insights. He helped organize the space. Within months, he was leading workshops—right there among the zucchini and compost bins.

Six months in, he told me, with a smile I hadn't seen before,

"It's strange, but I feel more useful now than I did in my last five years at the university."

He didn't find purpose by chasing status. He found it by showing up, staying open, and letting his gifts meet a need—no matter how small it seemed at first.

What Makes You Feel Useful?

If there's one question that consistently uncovers hidden purpose, it's this:

When do I feel most like myself—energized, alive, and contributing?

It's a deceptively simple question. But if you sit with it long enough, it can open the door to an entirely new way of living.

We've all had those moments—when time seemed to vanish, when we were "in the zone," fully immersed in something we cared about. Maybe it was helping someone solve a problem. Or organizing a family gathering. Maybe it was listening deeply to a friend, planting a garden, mentoring a young person, or creating something from nothing.

Those are moments of usefulness—but not the kind that comes from obligation. This kind of usefulness feels natural. It's not draining—it's energizing. It's not about proving something—it's about offering something.

And after those moments? You don't just feel accomplished. You feel aligned. You feel like yourself.

That's not an accident. That's your purpose trying to get your attention.

Tracing the Thread

Take a moment. Think back.

- When was the last time you felt fully present?

- What were you doing when you lost track of time?

- What activity left you feeling not just fulfilled, but joyful?

Now write it down. Don't edit. Don't judge. Just notice.

Now look for the thread that connects those moments. Ask yourself:

- What's the pattern here?

- Who am I when I'm doing this?

- What kind of energy does it require—and what kind does it return to me?

You may find that your moments of greatest usefulness have less to do with grand accomplishments and more to do with simple acts of connection, creativity, or care.

That's the beauty of this stage of life:

You no longer must be useful in the way the world defines it.

You get to redefine what usefulness looks and feels like for you.

Purpose Doesn't Have to Be Loud

One of the biggest misconceptions about purpose is that it has to be public, impressive, or tied to a platform. It doesn't.

Sometimes the most powerful contributions are the quietest:

- Walking your grandchild to school, and in doing so, becoming a stable, loving presence in their week.

- Helping a neighbor fix something they've been putting off—offering not just a helping hand, but dignity.

- Volunteering at a local shelter—not for recognition, but to remind someone else that they are seen and valued.

- Mentoring a young person over coffee, and realizing your wisdom still shapes the future.

- Writing your story—not because it'll be published, but because it matters to you, and it might matter to someone else one day.

- Being the person in your circle who listens—not to respond, but to truly understand.

These moments might not make headlines. But they make a difference.

And more importantly—they make you feel like you're living on purpose.

Follow That Feeling

If something makes you feel useful, alive, connected—pay attention to it.

Follow it. Honor it. Let it guide you.

That quiet sense of alignment you feel. That's your soul whispering, This is who I am. This is where I belong. This is what I still have to give.

And it doesn't need to be big to be beautiful.

Sometimes, the most sacred offerings we can make are the ones no one else sees. The kindness, the encouragement, the steady presence. These are not small things. These are seeds. And the harvest they produce may unfold in ways we never fully see—but deeply matter.

Ask yourself again, gently and honestly:

What makes me feel useful—not just in action, but in identity?

Let that question become your compass. Let it point you toward the people, places, and opportunities where you still have something meaningful to offer.

Because you do. You always have.

And in this new season of life, usefulness isn't about proving your worth—it's about living from it.

You're Not Starting Over. You're Starting with Wisdom.

Let me tell you something I wish every person entering retirement could hear—and believe:

You're not starting over.
You're starting with wisdom.

There's a huge difference.

Starting over implies that you're back at square one. That your past work, your life lessons, your scars, and triumphs somehow reset at zero the moment you hang up your work badge or close your office door for the last time.

That's simply not true.

You are not a blank slate—you're a living library.

You've lived. You've lost. You've loved. You've overcome.

You've navigated tough choices, learned hard lessons, and shaped lives—often without even realizing it.

That isn't baggage. That's treasure.

It's the kind of treasure that can't be bought, taught, or fast-tracked. It's only earned by showing up to life—over and over again.

And now, in this new season, you get to decide how you want to use that wisdom.

Not to impress anyone. Not to build a résumé. But to align your days with what really matters.

You Still Have Something to Offer

One of the quiet lies of aging is the idea that our most useful, impactful days are behind us. That once we retire from a position, we also retire from purpose. That once we leave the spotlight, we somehow leave relevance.

Don't buy that for a second.

The world may not always reflect it, but here's the truth:

We need your voice. We need your steadiness. We need your compassion, your discernment, your stories, your strength.

You carry something irreplaceable—not just knowledge, but perspective. Not just facts but understanding. Not just experience but earned wisdom.

The question isn't, "What role do I return to?"

The question is, "How can I share what I've become?"

That's the real gift of this season. You're not building a life out of ambition anymore—you're shaping it with intention.

Living from Overflow, Not Obligation

In this stage of life, purpose shifts. It no longer must come from pressure. It no longer needs to prove anything. And it certainly doesn't have to exhaust you.

This is your chance to live and give from overflow.

To serve not because someone expects it—but because it feels right.

To love not because you're supposed to—but because your heart is open and full.

To contribute not because it's on the calendar—but because it brings you joy.

It's the kind of freedom that comes when the need to perform falls away, and all that's left is authenticity.

This is what alignment feels like:

- Doing what matters to you

- In a way that honors who you are

- At a pace that nourishes you

There is no final exam in retirement. No one's grading your schedule.

You don't need to be impressive. You just need to be true.

Your Legacy Is Still Unfolding

Legacy isn't what you leave behind when you're gone. It's what you live into right now.

It's the lives you touch with your kindness.

The wisdom you offer in conversations.

The peace you carry into a room.

The example you set for how to live with integrity, even when no one's watching.

So don't think of this as a closing chapter.

Think of it as a deeper one.

The part of the story where the pace slows down, but the meaning runs deeper.

Where the spotlight softens, but the character development intensifies.

Where the best lines aren't written in bold—they're spoken quietly, with love.

Coming Next: Embracing the Power of Contribution

You don't need a job title to matter. You don't need a packed calendar to feel fulfilled.

What you do need is a sense of where your presence still makes a difference—and the courage to say yes to that.

In the next chapter, we'll explore what contribution really looks like in this season of life.

Not flashy. Not forced. But real.

Because when you begin to offer yourself with intention, the joy, connection, and purpose that follow aren't just fulfilling—they're life-giving.

Let's step into that space together.

Chapter 4

Embracing the Power of Contribution

You've done the work.

You've reflected. You've considered what purpose means for you now—not as a role assigned, but as a calling chosen.

So now comes the next powerful step: Contribution.

And let me be clear—when I say "contribution," I don't mean returning to the hustle. I'm not talking about filling your schedule to the brim or volunteering every hour of your week. This isn't about wearing yourself thin. This is about offering yourself intentionally.

Because here's the truth:

You were made to give. Not to prove your worth, but to express it.

I love this quote from Pablo Picasso:

"The meaning of life is to find your gift. The purpose of life is to give it away."

There is something hardwired into us—a quiet but persistent desire to matter, to make a difference, to pour into something beyond ourselves. That doesn't disappear with retirement. In fact, for many, it becomes more pronounced.

In the absence of deadlines and responsibilities, we start to ask:

- "Where do I still make a difference?"

- "How can I use what I've lived and learned to benefit someone else?"

- "What can I offer, not out of pressure, but out of joy?"

And the beautiful truth is—you don't need a title, a job, or an office to contribute in ways that change lives.

Sometimes, your presence is your power.

Contribution Is a State of Mind

We often associate contribution with big gestures—serving on boards, mentoring full-time, launching new projects. And those things are wonderful. But contribution also looks like:

- Making someone feel seen in the grocery store checkout line.

- Taking time to listen—really listen—when a friend is struggling.

- Holding space for your grandchildren to share their stories.

- Sending a note, offering a ride, showing up for someone who feels alone.

Small acts. Quiet moments. Ripples.

The difference is, in this stage of life, you're not contributing because it's on your job description.

You're doing it because it aligns with who you are and what you value.

You Don't Need Permission to Matter

There's no gatekeeper now. No one's assigning you tasks. And that can feel both freeing and unfamiliar.

But here's what I want you to remember:

You don't need permission to step into places where your presence makes a difference.

Your life has already given you everything you need to be of service to someone else:

- Your time

- Your empathy

- Your insight

- Your availability

- Your listening ear

- Your kindness

These are not small offerings. These are transformative.

And the best part? The more you give with intention, the more you receive in return. Not always in obvious ways—but in quiet joys, in deepened relationships, in the feeling that you are, once again, fully alive.

In this chapter, we'll explore the many forms of meaningful contribution—not out of obligation, but out of overflow.

Not as a duty—but as a gift.

Because when you show up in the world with a spirit of generosity, clarity, and love, something beautiful happens:

You become a living legacy.

Let's explore how to live that out—together.

The Shift from Achievement to Impact

There's a quiet—but profound—shift that begins to unfold when you leave your career behind. It doesn't happen all at once, and for some, it takes time to recognize. But eventually, the external noise softens, and a deeper voice begins to speak.

You move from chasing achievement to seeking impact.

For most of our working lives, achievement was how we measured progress. We set goals. We hit deadlines. We earned promotions, managed teams, launched projects, met budgets, and climbed ladders. We worked hard to reach tangible markers of success—and many of us did so very well.

But now? The scorecard changes.

Retirement brings a different kind of clarity. The applause fades. The reports stop coming. The metrics that once defined your days are no longer relevant. And that can feel strange, even disorienting—especially if your identity was deeply tied to accomplishment.

But here's the quiet beauty in that change: you are no longer defined by what you produce. You are free to be defined by what you contribute.

From Proving to Pouring

In your career, you may have often felt the need to prove yourself—to demonstrate your capability, leadership, or value. That pressure can drive performance, but it can also be exhausting.

Now, in this next chapter, you can pour yourself into what truly matters—not because you have something to prove, but because you have something to give.

Impact is no longer about how many people report to you. It's about how deeply you influence those around you.

It's about the friend who feels heard because you took time to listen.

The grandchild who remembers the way you showed up, consistently and lovingly.

The young professional who feels more confident because you shared your story and your encouragement.

These are not achievements in the traditional sense. You won't find them in an annual report. But they matter more than most of what ever did.

A Different Kind of Legacy

The impact you make now is often quieter—but more lasting. It's no longer measured in quarterly goals, but in the quality of your relationships, the wisdom you pass on, the presence you offer.

- It's found in the way you make someone feel seen.

- It's in the garden you tend, the meals you share, the stories you tell.

- It's in the encouragement you offer freely, without agenda.

- It's in the calm confidence that says, "You don't have to rush. I'm here."

You may not be at the front of the room anymore, but you still shape the room.

You may not be making headlines, but you're making memories.

You may not be running the meeting, but your example still speaks volumes.

This is the shift.

From performance to presence.

From pressure to purpose.

From measurable success to meaningful significance.

You Still Make a Difference—You Just Do It Differently Now

And perhaps the most important realization is this:

You still make a difference.

You just do it differently now.

You're not building systems—you're building people.

You're not scaling strategies—you're deepening lives.

You're not chasing titles—you're chasing truth, connection, and joy.

And isn't that the point of it all?

Embrace the shift. Let go of the need to perform and lean into the gift of presence. Your impact may not be as loud as it once was, but it's more lasting, more human, and more sacred than ever before.

What Do You Still Have to Give?

Let me ask you a question that often brings a long pause, a deep breath, and sometimes even tears:

"What do you still have to give that the world needs?"

It's not a question about filling time. It's not about being busy or productive in the way we used to measure those things.

This is a question about meaning. About service. About the quiet usefulness that brings you back to life.

Because the truth is—no matter your age, stage, or status—you still have something to give. Something real. Something needed. Something only you can offer, with your unique mix of life experience, personality, and perspective.

The Surprising Desire to Be Needed

Let me tell you about someone who reminded me just how deep this desire goes.

She was a high-achieving healthcare executive—smart, driven, respected. She retired early, financially set, ready to enjoy the life she had worked hard to build.

At first, she did all the right things. She traveled, tackled home projects, joined a few clubs. On paper, it looked like the dream.

But when we sat down six months after she stepped away from her career, she surprised me. She said:

"I thought I'd feel free. But what I really feel... is like I'm not useful anymore."

Not useful. Not needed. Not contributing in a way that felt meaningful.

She wasn't missing meetings or reports. She didn't want to go back to 60-hour weeks. What she missed was the feeling of making someone else's life just a little better.

We started exploring. What did she love most about her work—not the title, but the actual experience? She spoke about helping patients navigate confusing systems. She talked about listening to scared families and mentoring younger staff. That's where the spark lived.

And then something beautiful happened.

She found a small community health clinic in her city. They needed someone to help at the front desk—nothing glamorous. Intake paperwork. Translation support. Simple patient navigation.

She showed up once a week. No title. No decision-making power. No executive role.

But within weeks, she told me:

"I feel like I've come home to myself."

She didn't need to lead the room to light it up.

She didn't need authority to offer compassion.

She didn't need a paycheck to make a difference.

You Still Have So Much to Offer

And so do you.

Your contributions don't have to look the same as they did in your professional life. They may be quieter now. More relational. More intuitive. But make no mistake—they are no less powerful.

You still have:

- A lifetime of wisdom

- The ability to listen deeply

- The courage to show up

- Compassion that only grows with time

- Calming presence others desperately need

- Creativity that can't be automated

- A voice that someone is waiting to hear

And you don't have to be center stage to offer it. Some of the most lasting impact comes from simply being present, being kind, and being available—for the people and causes that speak to your heart.

Let the Question Lead You

So let me ask again—and this time, maybe write down what comes:

What do I still have to give that the world needs?

Start with small, honest answers. You don't need a five-year plan. You just need a place to begin.

Maybe it's mentoring.

Maybe it's art.

Maybe it's laughter.

Maybe it's patience.

Maybe it's simply showing up when others don't.

But whatever it is—it matters.

You still have so much to give.

And the world still needs your light, your wisdom, your hands, and your heart.

Don't Underestimate the Small Moments

In a world that often glorifies big achievements, it's easy to forget something essential:

Contribution doesn't have to be loud to be lasting.

It doesn't need to be wrapped in titles or announcements. It doesn't have to trend on social media or show up in a quarterly report. In fact, some of the most powerful contributions you'll ever make won't look like much from the outside.

They'll be small. Ordinary, even. But they will carry enormous weight in someone else's life.

It might look like:

- A handwritten note to someone who's grieving, offering not solutions, but presence.

- Sitting with a friend who just needs someone to listen—really listen—without rushing in to fix anything.

- Mentoring a young leader who's facing challenges you remember all too well.

- Cooking a meal for a neighbor going through a tough time, simply because it's what you would want someone to do for you.

- Dropping off a book to someone who's had a hard week. Calling a friend "just because." Showing up to support someone else's dream.

These are the quiet moments. The unscheduled, unmeasured offerings of the heart.

And yet, they're often the ones people remember most.

The Sacredness of the Simple

One of the unexpected—and beautiful—gifts of retirement is this:

You're no longer too busy to notice the sacredness of the simple.

In our working years, we were often moving so fast, we didn't have time to slow down and offer those small gestures. Not because we didn't care, but because there just wasn't space.

Now, there is. And that space is precious.

You have time to be thoughtful. To follow a nudge. To pause, reach out, and offer something—without fanfare, and without needing to multitask your way through it.

These are the moments where meaning lives:

- In eye contact.

- In a well-timed hug.

- In being willing to sit in silence with someone who doesn't yet have words for their pain.

- In showing up—not because you have to, but because you want to.

And here's the incredible part: these small moments are often where healing happens.

You may never know the full impact of the kindness you offer. But that doesn't make it any less real. In fact, that quiet anonymity might be what makes it sacred.

It's the Little Things That Build a Life

At the end of our lives, we likely won't recount the number of meetings we led or emails we sent.

We'll remember—and be remembered for—the small, human acts that shaped someone's day:

- The call that came at just the right moment

- The unexpected encouragement that kept someone going

- The kindness that softened someone's hard season

- The steady presence that made someone feel safe and seen

So please—don't underestimate the power of what you might call "small."

Because what may seem small to you might feel enormous to someone else.

The next time you wonder, "Am I doing enough?"—remember this:

You don't have to do everything. You just have to do what's in front of you, with heart.

That's more than enough.

That's legacy.

That's love in motion.

Define Your Personal Contribution Zone

Here's a simple way to discover where you might contribute now:

1. What are you naturally good at? Listening, encouraging, organizing, teaching?

2. Who or what breaks your heart or lights you up? That's where your compassion lives.

3. Where do you have margin? Not just time—but energy.

The intersection of those three? That's your Contribution Zone.

You don't need a resume. You need willingness.

Contribution = Connection

Here's something we often overlook contribution is as much for you as it is for others.

Why? Because when you contribute, you feel connected.

- To purpose
- To people
- To your own sense of value

You start to remember that you still matter. That your presence has weight. That even if the phone isn't ringing every hour, you're still needed.

Coming Next: Navigating the Emotional Undercurrents of Retirement

Because even with purpose and structure, this chapter can stir up unexpected emotions—grief, loss, confusion, joy. And that's okay. Let's make space for all of it.

Chapter 5

The Emotional Undercurrents

No One Warns You About This Part

You spend months—sometimes years—getting ready for retirement.

You meet with your financial planner. You run the numbers again (just to be sure). You research Medicare options, finalize paperwork, and maybe even book a celebratory trip. The spreadsheets are tidy. The estate plan is signed. The send-off party is scheduled.

And then, just like that, it's here.

The inbox clears.

The meetings disappear.

The calendar breathes.

There's a toast, a few speeches, a thoughtful gift from your team. You shake hands, exchange hugs, maybe even shed a tear or two. People say kind things. You nod, smile, and walk into your new season with your head held high.

And for a little while, everything feels just as it should. The quiet feels like relief. The mornings feel luxurious. The lack of urgency feels like a long-overdue gift.

But then—slowly, quietly—something begins to shift.

The days get longer.

The to-do list gets shorter.

The silence gets louder.

The Unexpected Ache

You don't notice it right away.

Maybe it shows up in the stillness of your living room, where your phone used to buzz with updates and reminders.

Maybe it creeps in during a Tuesday afternoon, when you realize you haven't spoken to another adult all day.

Maybe it settles in your chest as you look at a wide-open week and wonder: What do I even want to do with all this time?

It's not overwhelming. It's not dramatic. It's not something you'd mention in casual conversation.

But it's there.

A flicker of sadness you can't quite explain.

A strange restlessness in your body.

A quiet thought that whispers when things get too still:

"Why don't I feel better?"

This was supposed to be the good part—the reward for all those years of showing up, grinding it out, pushing forward.

And in many ways, it is the good part. But it's also something else:

It's the invisible part no one really talks about.

The emotional undercurrent that doesn't show up on your retirement checklist.

The tender truth that even a beautiful transition can come with grief.

The Quiet That Reveals

Here's what I've learned:

Beneath all the freedom and possibility of retirement—beneath the invitations to travel, volunteer, or take up a new hobby—there's often something deeper stirring.

An ache. A disorientation. A soft sense of being unmoored.

You've stepped out of the current of daily obligations, but the current hasn't quite let go of you. Your body still wakes up on schedule. Your brain still searches for urgency. Your heart still longs to be useful, to be seen.

And when those things aren't immediately present—when the noise of the job is replaced by the spaciousness of your home—the silence can feel less like peace and more like absence.

It's not that something is wrong.

It's that something important has changed.

When Stillness Surprises You

Stillness sounds so appealing until you're in it.

Until the applause fades.

Until the last congratulatory card is tucked away.

Until the rhythm you once knew so well is replaced by… what, exactly?

For many people, this season brings a collision of opposites:

- Gratitude and grief

- Peace and purposelessness

- Joy and guilt

- Rest and restlessness

And that emotional mix can be disorienting.

You begin to realize that you didn't just retire from your job.

You retired from a way of being—a way of knowing yourself.

And now you're faced with the unfamiliar challenge of reinventing that self-outside the framework of productivity and achievement.

Why We Must Name It

This chapter is about that moment. The one few people prepare you for.

Because if we don't name what's happening—if we pretend everything's fine, if we fill every quiet space with distraction or busyness—we miss the opportunity for real transformation.

We miss the chance to:

- Mourn what's been lost

- Understand what's shifting

- And choose, with intention, what comes next

The emotional undercurrent of retirement isn't something to resist.

It's something to respect.

Because underneath the ache is an invitation.

An invitation to feel. To reimagine. To rebuild.

And like all invitations, you don't have to accept it all at once.

You just have to start by saying, "This matters too."

Loss That Doesn't Look Like Loss

Here's what most people don't tell you: retirement, even when it's planned, chosen, and eagerly anticipated, comes with loss.

But it's not always a visible, nameable kind of loss.

It's not as dramatic as a funeral. But it still hurts. And that pain deserves attention.

You've lost more than just a paycheck.

- You've lost structure—the rhythm and routine that once anchored your days.

- You've lost your title—the identity that helped people understand who you were.

- You've lost your team—the people who needed you, relied on you, challenged you.

- You've lost your role in a system—the meetings, the emails, the phone calls, the problems that needed solving.

You may have even lost your sense of momentum. Of being "in motion." Of being someone who mattered in a specific way.

It's easy to overlook this kind of loss because it doesn't always come with sympathy cards or casseroles. But grief isn't reserved for death. Grief belongs to every meaningful ending. And retirement, in many ways, is an ending.

Not of life.

But of a chapter you gave decades of your energy to.

And letting that chapter go—even to embrace a good one—still requires courage.

The Emotional Whirlwind

Let's talk about the experience no one prepares you for.

You close the door on your career, wake up the next morning without an alarm, and somewhere between the first sip of coffee and the second week of unstructured days, something stirs.

You're not falling apart—but your emotions might be taking you on a ride you didn't expect.

Here are just a few of the things I've heard from people in their first year of retirement:

- Relief: "Finally. No more meetings. No more deadlines. I can breathe again."

- Boredom: "It felt good for a few weeks. Then I started wondering what to do with myself."

- Gratitude: "I feel lucky to be here. So many people never make it to this stage."

- Anxiety: "What if I made a mistake? What if I run out of money? Out of meaning?"

- Emptiness: "I didn't expect to miss being needed. But I do."

- Joy: "I get to choose how I spend my time. That freedom feels incredible."

- Guilt: "I thought I'd be doing more. Giving more. I feel like I'm not contributing enough."

- Shame: "I'm embarrassed to admit I miss the structure of work. I didn't think I would."

- Restlessness: "I feel like I'm supposed to be relaxing, but something in me wants to move—to do something that matters."

If that list feels contradictory, confusing, or even overwhelming… good. It should.

Because retirement doesn't unfold in a neat emotional sequence. There's no predictable path where relief is followed by joy, followed by purpose, followed by peace.

Retirement is messy.

Retirement is layered.

Retirement is human.

It's more like the weather than a checklist.

One morning you wake up and feel a lightness in your chest—hopeful, grateful, ready to seize the day.

By noon, you're knee-deep in a cloud of self-doubt, wondering if you're doing any of this "right."

By evening, you've had a beautiful conversation with an old friend and feel grounded again.

Sunshine. Thunderstorm. Calm skies.

All in one day.

And here's the thing: that's normal.

That's what change feels like—not on paper, but in real life.

Why These Emotions Matter

The emotions that rise up in retirement aren't signs of failure.

They're invitations.

Each one is trying to tell you something.

- Relief tells you that the pace you were keeping might not have been sustainable.

- Boredom is your spirit whispering, "I'm ready for something meaningful."

- Gratitude is the grounding force that reminds you how much you already have.

- Anxiety is a signal to slow down and create clarity.

- Emptiness reveals that fulfillment was once tied to things that have changed—and that it's time to redefine it.

- Joy reminds you that you still know how to come alive.

- Guilt and shame show up when we internalize outdated expectations about what retirement should look like.

- Restlessness is your soul asking, "What's next?"

Every one of these emotions carries information.

None of them are wrong.

They're simply part of the landscape of becoming someone new.

Let Yourself Ride the Weather

If you've ever lived through a long storm or a surprising weather shift, you know how nature works.

It doesn't ask your permission.

It doesn't follow your schedule.

It simply moves through.

Emotions in retirement are a lot like that.

They move in. They hang around. And eventually, if you allow them to have their space, they move out. Sometimes slowly. Sometimes suddenly. Sometimes they circle back just when you thought you were in the clear.

But the key is this:

Don't resist the weather. Learn to ride it.

Let the rain come when it needs to. Let the clouds pass. Let the sun surprise you.

The more you resist the emotional tides of retirement, the more disoriented you'll feel. But the more you allow yourself to feel everything, the more grounded you'll become.

Because these emotions aren't obstacles to joy—they're pathways to it.

The emotional whirlwind isn't a detour. It is the road.

And once you accept that, you'll start to see that even the hardest days are part of the process of becoming more fully yourself.

And the goal isn't to "fix" those feelings.

It's to feel them. To welcome them.

To understand that emotions are not signs you're failing at retirement—they're signs that you're human and transitioning through something important.

You Are Not Broken—You're Becoming

One of the most tender truths I can offer you in this chapter of your life is this:

You're not broken. You're becoming.

Let those words settle for a moment.

If you're feeling wobbly, uncertain, or disoriented—if your days feel like a mix of quiet joy and quiet unease—it doesn't mean something is wrong with you.

It means something important is changing in you.

You're not lost.

You're in transition.

And transitions are not tidy. They are transformational.

Think about what's really happening beneath the surface.

You're no longer wearing the titles that once defined you. The ones printed on business cards or spoken at meetings. The ones that answered the question, "So, what do you do?" before you even had to think.

You're no longer on the clock, no longer in motion out of necessity. And with that freedom comes something unexpected: the need to relearn how to be—not for others, but for yourself.

You are learning how to stand in your life as you are now— without the scaffolding of roles, routines, or recognition.

That takes time.

And it takes courage.

You've stepped away from the identity that guided you for decades—and even if you did so by choice, there's still grief in that. There's still uncertainty. And there's often a deep, quiet question lingering beneath it all:

Who am I without that version of me?

And the answer—if you're willing to be patient—is this:

You're someone who is still unfolding.

Still discovering.

Still capable of surprising yourself.

Transitions like this are deeply human experiences. They are on par with other major life thresholds—becoming a parent, losing a loved one, going through divorce, moving to a new place. We often talk about these events with reverence and weight. Retirement deserves the same kind of space.

Because just like those moments, retirement asks you to reconfigure your sense of self.

To set down one story so you can begin writing another.

And just like with any story shift, you might fumble with the pen at first. You might stare at the blank page, unsure how to begin.

That's okay.

This is not a race.

It's a restoration.

So please—extend to yourself the same grace you'd offer a close friend.

If your friend were adjusting to a major life change, would you rush them?

Would you tell them to figure it out faster, to feel something different to "just get over it"?

Of course not.

You'd sit with them. You'd listen. You'd tell them they're doing better than they think.

That's the same kindness you deserve.

You don't need a blueprint. You need breath.

You don't need answers. You need permission—to be in process.

And if that feels hard, here's something that might help.

Honor, Then Release

There's an exercise I've shared with many people in this stage of life. And I've done it myself, more than once. It's simple, but it holds deep power:

Write a letter to the version of yourself who lived the first act.

The version who rose early, stayed late, carried the weight of deadlines and expectations.

The one who built things—careers, homes, teams, families.

The one who held it together, who stretched, who sacrificed, who showed up again and again.

Write to that person. And in that letter:

- Honor them. Tell them what you're proud of.

- Thank them. Acknowledge what they endured, what they contributed, what they made possible.

- Recognize them. The late nights. The hard choices. The victories and the wounds.

And then—when you've said what needs saying—release them.

Close the letter not with goodbye, but with gratitude.

"Thank you. You got me here. Now it's time for me to keep going."

Let that version of you rest—not erased, but integrated.

Not dismissed but given a place of honor on your internal shelf.

Because you're not abandoning who you were.

You're building on it. You're expanding it.

You're becoming someone new—not instead of who you've been, but because of who you've been.

That's what this season is about.

Becoming isn't flashy. It's not always Instagram-worthy or celebrated at dinner parties.

Sometimes it looks like taking a slow walk by yourself.

Sometimes it feels like crying unexpectedly in the grocery store.

Sometimes it's an early morning cup of coffee and a feeling that maybe, you're starting to feel a little more like you again.

And over time, as you continue to show up—with compassion, curiosity, and courage—

you begin to realize:

You are not broken.

You are healing.

You are growing.

You are becoming someone beautifully aligned with who you were always meant to be.

Let Yourself Feel It All

Here's what I've come to believe—after countless conversations, after walking this road myself, and after listening to people who've found real peace in their second act:

The people who truly thrive in retirement aren't the ones who outrun the emotional messiness.
They're the ones who have the courage to walk straight into it—with honesty, compassion, and grace.

They slow down enough to feel everything that's rising—without judgment, without shame.

They let the tears come when they miss the office chatter or the sense of being needed.

They let the smiles surface when they remember how far they've come.

They let the confusion breathe, instead of burying it under productivity or distraction.

They:

• Grieve what's gone—honoring the chapters that shaped them, even as they turn the page.

• Celebrate what was—without minimizing it or clinging to it too tightly.

• Sit in the in-between—without needing to fix it right away or wrap it in a bow.

• Begin again—with eyes wide open, a softened heart, and the willingness to live differently.

It takes real strength to feel it all.

To stand still when everything in you wants to rush ahead.

To resist the urge to "get over it" and instead move through it.

We live in a culture that often encourages avoidance—scroll past the sadness, stay busy, keep it light. But growth doesn't happen in avoidance. It happens in presence.

In pausing long enough to ask: What am I really feeling here? And what might that feeling be trying to teach me?

When you do this, when you welcome your emotions like houseguests instead of intruders, something begins to shift. You realize you're not broken—you're becoming. You're not unraveling—you're realigning.

You stop trying to rush back to who you were and start getting curious about who you're becoming.

And here's the beautiful surprise:

When you give your inner life the attention it deserves, your outer life starts to settle.

- You stop reacting from fear and start responding from wisdom.

- You start finding meaning in places you once overlooked.

- You begin to feel a quiet confidence return—not because everything is certain, but because you're okay being uncertain for a while.

This is when something deeper than peace emerges.

You begin to feel alignment—that sense that your inner world and outer life are starting to reflect one another.

You begin to feel clarity—not in the form of a grand plan, but in the simplicity of knowing what matters most.

And perhaps most important of all,

You begin to feel yourself again.
Not the version shaped by decades of doing and achieving.
But the version that is grounded, wise, human, and alive.

That's the true work of this season—not to pretend everything is perfect, but to grow strong enough to feel everything that comes your way and still move forward with an open heart.

So let yourself feel it all.

You're not falling apart.

You're coming together in a new way.

Coming Next: Relationships in Transition

Retirement doesn't just change your schedule—it changes your connections.

Because when your rhythm shifts, your relationships often shift too—at home, in friendships, in how you show up for others and how you need them to show up for you.

That change can be awkward. Or beautiful. Often both.

But if you're willing to explore it, it can become one of the most rewarding parts of this second act.

Let's go there next.

Chapter 6
Relationships in Transition

When you step into retirement, you're not the only one going through a change.

Your schedule shifts. Your identity shifts. And inevitably—your relationships shift, too.

Sometimes the changes are subtle.

Other times they're unmistakably loud.

Either way, they matter.

Because for years—decades even—your life had a built-in rhythm of connection. Whether it was morning meetings, hallway conversations, client check-ins, classroom energy, or the simple ritual of commuting with familiar faces, you had a place in the flow of social life.

Even if those connections weren't deeply personal, they were constant.

They were woven into the fabric of your days.

And then—suddenly—quiet.

The meetings stop.

The phone doesn't ring as often.

The inbox empties.

The people you once interacted with daily are still in motion…

and you're not.

And it's in that unexpected quiet that a new question often rises to the surface:

"Where do I belong now?"

The Social Cliff

There's a moment that catches many people off guard—not with a bang, but with a slow, steady silence.

It happens after the farewell toasts have been made, after your last calendar meeting has been marked as "completed," after the stream of daily emails begins to dry up.

Suddenly, the rhythm of interaction you once took for granted is gone.

And what replaces it isn't always peace. Sometimes, it's a profound and unexpected void.

Researchers have given this moment a name:

The Social Cliff of Retirement.

It's the sharp drop-off in daily interpersonal connection that occurs when you step away from the structured relationships of work. One day, your life is full of scheduled conversations, impromptu check-ins, shared deadlines, and hallway updates. The next, your phone stays quiet. The office chatter fades. The world moves on—and it can feel like it left you standing at the edge of something vast and undefined.

When the Energy of Connection Disappears

The social cliff doesn't mean you're completely alone. But it does mean your ecosystem of connection—the people who filled your days, the casual relationships that gave your routine texture—has changed dramatically.

And you may find yourself grieving things you never thought you'd miss:

- The casual back-and-forth in a morning meeting
- The random drop-ins at your office door
- The shared sense of urgency around a deadline
- The mutual eyeroll with a coworker after a long Zoom call
- Even the mildly annoying team member who somehow made your day more interesting

These weren't just people.

They were part of your social scaffolding.

They were the daily affirmations that said, You're here. You're part of something. You're needed.

So, when that structure disappears, it's not unusual to feel untethered. Even invisible.

It's not just the job that's gone. It's the way people saw you. It's the part of you that knew where you fit.

You Are Not Unseen—You're in Transition

This shift can feel subtle at first. A slow drift, not a free fall.

You realize the phone rings less.

Fewer texts come in.

You no longer run into people in the breakroom or walk to lunch with a colleague who always made you laugh.

And while some friendships from work may survive the transition, many will fade—not because they weren't real, but because they were rooted in a shared environment that no longer exists.

That disconnection doesn't mean those relationships weren't meaningful.

It simply means they belonged to a different chapter of your life.

Now, the pages are turning—and that's where the good news begins:

This disconnection is not a dead end. It's an invitation.

Your Circle Is Yours to Redefine

Retirement offers you something most people only dream about:

The freedom to choose your people.

No more office politics.

No more proximity-based friendships that drain your energy.

No more spending time with people because you "should."

You get to ask better questions now:

- Who fills me up instead of depleting me?
- Who challenges me in a way that feels respectful and life-giving?
- Who brings out the version of me I like?

That's who you build your circle around.

You may carry a handful of meaningful relationships forward from your career—and that's a gift. But you'll likely find that others fade away. That's not a failure. That's just life doing what life does—evolving.

Some connections were made for a moment.

Others are meant to carry forward.

And now, you get to choose which is which.

Don't Build a Bigger Circle—Build a Deeper One

This next season isn't about collecting more contacts.

It's about cultivating more meaning.

You're not networking.

You're building a life.

A life made richer by people who:
- Listen without judgment
- Share your values or expand your worldview
- Laugh with you, walk with you, sit quietly with you
- See you—not for your résumé, but for your presence

This is a chance to build your relationships not around convenience, but around curiosity and kindness.

You don't need everyone to like you.

You need a few people who truly know you.

You don't need to be busy to feel important.

You need to feel connected—in ways that nourish your soul, not just fill your calendar.

Presence Over Performance

In this new season, let your guiding principle be this:

Presence over performance. Depth over display. Joy over obligation.

Your time is now your own.

Give it to the people who reflect your truest self back to you.

Give it to conversations that spark something meaningful.

Give it to spaces that feel sacred—not because they're fancy, but because they're real.

This is your chance to redefine not just who you're with—but how you show up.

Because sometimes, when the scaffolding falls away, you finally see what's meant to be built in its place.

And trust me: what you build from here—intentionally, slowly, authentically—will last longer and feel deeper than anything proximity ever created.

At Home: A New Dance

Now let's talk about the people closest to you—not your former colleagues, not your casual friends, but the ones under your own roof.

Because retirement doesn't just shift your social circles—it reshapes your home life.

And for many couples, it's one of the most surprising, and at times, most tender parts of the transition.

Together… A Lot More Than Before

When one person retires while the other continues working, a new imbalance forms. One partner is adjusting to open time and newfound freedom. The other is still bound by routines and expectations. And that mismatch can lead to confusion or even quiet resentment if it isn't acknowledged.

But even when both people retire together, it's not all leisurely breakfasts and long walks hand-in-hand.

Because suddenly… you're in each other's space.

All. The. Time.

The rhythm of "see you tonight" becomes "you again already?"

The empty nest doesn't feel so empty anymore.

The living room becomes a shared workspace.

And lunch, once a quick break alone, becomes a twice-daily negotiation about who's cooking.

None of this is bad.

But it is new.

And new rhythms, like any good dance, require practice.

You have to learn how to move with each other in this new season—not just physically, but emotionally.

The Myth of Constant Togetherness

There's a romantic ideal many people carry into retirement:

"Now that we're both home, we'll do everything together!"

It sounds lovely. But it's not always realistic—or healthy.

Because while togetherness is beautiful, individuality still matters.

You both need:

- Purpose: something that's just yours
- Space: time apart to breathe, reflect, or simply be
- Voice: the ability to express how you're really feeling in this new chapter

Without clear communication, the very closeness you craved can start to feel constricting.

Without permission to have separate interests, even the strongest relationships can fray at the edges.

That's why honest, kind conversations are the heartbeat of this dance.

The Conversation That Changes Everything

One of the most powerful questions I encourage couples to ask each other in this season is simple:

"What does a good day look like for you in this season—and how can I support it?"

Not what should we do today?

Not what do you need from me?

But what feels good and meaningful to you now?

This question opens space to talk about what matters.

It invites the other person to be seen not as your mirror, but as their own person.

It removes pressure and replaces it with curiosity.

And the answers?

They might surprise you.

You might learn that your partner needs more quiet than you realized.

Or more companionship.

Or time in the garden, or a project of their own, or simply a little structure to feel grounded.

And by asking—and truly listening—you begin to dance with each other in a way that honors not just your shared life, but your separate growth.

The Joy of Learning New Steps

Like any dance, this one requires flexibility.

Some days you'll move together in sync, naturally and effortlessly.

Other days you'll step on each other's toes. You'll misread the rhythm. You'll need to pause and try again.

That's okay. That's part of it.

The couples who thrive in retirement are not the ones who avoid tension.

They're the ones who stay curious about each other. Who give each other room to evolve. Who ask the better questions and adjust their steps with grace.

Because retirement isn't just about adjusting your schedule.

It's about reimagining your life together—in all its messiness, beauty, and surprise.

So be patient.

With your partner. With yourself. With the process.

This dance is not about perfection.

It's about presence.

It's about making room for each other—not just physically, but emotionally.

And when you do that?

The dance becomes not just bearable, but joyful.

You rediscover why you chose each other in the first place.

And you find new reasons to fall in love—with this season, with each other, and with the person you're both still becoming.

Loneliness Is Not a Weakness

If you find yourself feeling lonely in retirement—please, hear this loud and clear:

You are not weak. You are not failing. You are human.

Really take that in.

Because somewhere along the way, we've been taught that loneliness is a sign of personal failure. That if you feel isolated, it must be because you didn't "build your life right." That if you're longing for connection, you must be doing retirement wrong.

Nothing could be further from the truth.

The truth is:

We are wired for connection.

It's part of our biology, our psychology, and our spirituality.

And when that connection shifts—when daily interactions fade, when routines dissolve, when the people who filled our lives with conversation and collaboration are no longer in reach—it impacts us on a deep level.

Not just socially.

Not just logistically.

But spiritually—in the part of us that longs to be seen, known, and valued.

Loneliness Doesn't Always Look Like What You Think

It's not always stark or dramatic.

Sometimes it's subtle:

- A quiet ache that lingers, even on peaceful days
- A vague restlessness you can't quite name
- A sense that something's missing, even though everything "looks good" on paper
- An emotional fog that rolls in around midafternoon and stays through dinner

It can feel like being surrounded by people, yet not truly connected to any of them.

It can feel like checking your phone more often, hoping someone thought of you.

It can feel like wondering, "Does anyone really know what I'm going through?"

Loneliness wears many faces. And it doesn't care how "together" your life looks from the outside.

Reach Out Anyway

One of the hardest things about loneliness is that it can convince you to withdraw even more.

It whispers, "Don't bother anyone."

"They're probably busy."

"You shouldn't need this much connection."

But that voice is not your truth. It's just fear dressed up as pride.

So don't wait for others to notice your silence.

Be the one who reaches out:
- Send a simple text to an old friend
- Invite someone for a walk or coffee
- Share something personal and honest with someone you trust

- Join a group, even if you feel unsure walking in the first time

It takes vulnerability to go first.

But vulnerability builds bridges.

And more often than not, the person you reach out to is feeling something similar—and just waiting for an invitation.

Creating New Circles

You don't have to rebuild your entire social world overnight.

This isn't a race or a project to manage.

It's a quiet practice of staying open to connection—wherever it may come from.

Here are a few simple ways I've seen retirees create meaningful, soul-filling connection:

- Start a "Third Act" small group — focused on purpose, books, creativity, or shared reflection. You don't need a fancy format—just a reason to gather and grow.
- Volunteer with others — not just solo. Find places where contribution and camaraderie go hand in hand.

- Mentor someone younger — personally or professionally. You have more wisdom to offer than you think, and someone out there needs your voice.
- Join a class, workshop, or community group that stretches your curiosity and introduces you to people outside your usual orbit.
- Reconnect with someone from your past — someone you always liked, but life never gave you the time to deepen the relationship.

Sometimes new circles come from new communities.

Other times, they come from rediscovering people who were already there.

This Isn't About Staying Busy

Let's be clear: this isn't about filling your time for the sake of distraction.

This isn't about being constantly social or pushing past your need for solitude.

This is about staying connected:

- To yourself
- To people who see and celebrate you
- To the flow of life that reminds you you're not alone

It's about belonging—not just somewhere, but with someone.

It's about knowing that your presence, your story, and your heart are still needed in the world.

If loneliness comes knocking, don't shame yourself.

Welcome it like a signal—a gentle tap on the shoulder saying:

"You're ready for more connection. Go find it."

Because it's out there.

And when you take that first step, you won't just ease the ache...

You'll expand your life in ways you never expected.

The Gift of Presence

Here's something you might not realize—especially if you've spent most of your life being recognized for what you do:

Your presence still carries weight.

Not your résumé.

Not your role.

Not your productivity.

You. Just you.

When you step away from the career stage—from the meetings, the deadlines, the titles, the daily responsibilities—it's easy to wonder, "Do I still matter in the same way?"

The answer is yes.

In fact, sometimes you matter more—because your presence is no longer transactional.

It's intentional.

You're no longer showing up out of obligation or expectation.

You're showing up because you choose to. And that choice carries power.

No Title Required

Let's clear something up: You don't need a business card to be valuable.

You don't need a corner office or a job title to have impact.

In fact, some of the most meaningful influence you'll have in this chapter of life comes not from your credentials—but from your character.

The people around you—your family, your neighbors, your community, even strangers you might cross paths with—don't need you to perform.

They need you to be present.

Fully there. Fully engaged. Fully you.

The Simple Power of Being There

Sometimes, the most powerful gift you can give another person is your attention.

- The way you sit and actually listen without trying to fix or impress.
- The way you laugh at just the right moment and lighten the air in the room.
- The way your calm steadiness reassures others that everything is going to be okay.
- The way your presence says: You matter. I see you. I'm here.

You don't need to lead a meeting to lead a moment.

You don't need to deliver a speech to speak wisdom.

You don't need to be "in charge" to have influence.

Still in Rooms That Matter

You may no longer be in boardrooms or classrooms or daily operations—but you are still in rooms that matter deeply:

- Around the dinner table with a grandchild who needs your stories more than you know.

- At the community center where a warm smile or a curious question makes someone feel seen.
- In a quiet kitchen, sharing coffee and presence with a friend navigating a loss.
- On a walk, where your patient listening gives someone space to speak freely for the first time in weeks.

These aren't "small" things.

They're sacred things.

Because in a noisy, fast-moving world, presence has become one of the rarest and most powerful gifts we can offer.

Presence Leaves a Legacy

One day, people won't remember your job title.

They may not remember your career highlights or your accomplishments on paper.

But they will remember how you made them feel.

They'll remember the day you showed up when you didn't have to.

They'll remember the warmth of your voice, the steadiness of your encouragement, the way you listened with your eyes and your heart.

That's the kind of legacy that lasts.

Presence isn't just about being in the room.

It's about bringing your full self into the room—open, available, real.

And that, my friend, is something the world needs now more than ever.

So don't underestimate yourself in this season.

Your presence may not come with applause.

It may not earn awards.

But it will make a difference—in ways that are deep, enduring, and sometimes invisible until much later.

Keep showing up.

Keep offering your attention.

Keep choosing presence over performance.

Because you still matter.

And every room you enter is better because you walked into it.

Coming Next: Staying Sharp—Mind, Body, and Spirit

Because connection is essential—but so is the energy that sustains it.

And the truth is, the more you care for your body, your mind, and your soul, the more fully you can show up—for yourself and for those you love.

Let's explore how to keep that energy alive.

Chapter 7
Staying Sharp—Mind, Body, and Spirit

There's a funny myth about retirement.

People assume it's your permission slip to coast.

To exchange the treadmill of your working life for the recliner of rest.

To replace the alarm clock with a lazy sunrise and trade hustle for hammock.

And let's be honest—some of that is deserved.

After years of showing up, giving your all, and living by other people's timelines, you should have mornings that begin slow, afternoons that include a nap, and evenings without pressure.

Rest is sacred. It's earned. And it's essential.

But rest isn't the opposite of energy.

And retirement isn't the finish line.

It's a launch pad.

This new season of life isn't just about what you're stepping away from.

It's about what you're stepping into.

Not just freedom from the clock or the commute—but the freedom to tune into yourself in a way that your previous life never quite allowed.

The freedom to ask:

- What brings me life?
- What makes me feel engaged?
- What helps me feel most me?

The answer to all of those starts with one powerful principle:

Staying sharp.

Not just mentally, but emotionally, physically, and spiritually.

Because how you take care of yourself now won't just shape how long you live—it will shape how fully you live.

The Shift from Pushing to Tuning

During your working years, you were likely a master of the push.

Pushing through the deadlines.

Pushing past exhaustion.

Pushing for progress.

Your schedule dictated your energy, and your energy had no choice but to obey.

But retirement? Retirement offers you something entirely new:

The space to stop pushing and start tuning in.

Tuning in doesn't mean slacking off.

It means paying attention.

It means learning the subtle rhythms of your own body, your own creativity, your own emotional and spiritual needs—and responding to them with care, not control.

It means asking questions like:

- What energizes me now?
- What drains me—even if it didn't used to?
- What makes me feel aligned, alive, and awake?

This isn't about meeting a goal. It's about meeting yourself, where you are now.

Because staying sharp is not about proving anything.

It's about feeling well enough to enjoy everything.

Mental Vitality: Keep Learning, Keep Wondering

Let's begin with your mind—your capacity for thought, imagination, memory, and curiosity.

The brain, like any muscle, doesn't like stagnation.

It thrives on challenge, variety, stimulation. And the good news?

You don't need exams or textbooks. You need curiosity.

In fact, the most powerful thing you can ask yourself is:

"What am I learning right now that actually matters to me?"

Notice: not should I learn but want to learn.

Because now, for the first time in a long time, you don't have to absorb knowledge out of obligation.

You get to pursue learning for the joy of it.

Here are a few meaningful ways to keep your mind agile:

- Take a class—in person or online—on something that's always intrigued you
- Join a book group, or better yet, start one with a few friends
- Write regularly—in a journal, a blog, a notebook of life lessons you want to pass on
- Learn a new skill, not to perform, but to play—cooking, painting, photography, coding, quilting
- Travel with intention, not just to see new sights but to open new windows into different ways of living

This isn't about being busy for the sake of it.

It's about being engaged.

Because engagement fuels your sense of purpose.

Purpose sparks interest.

And interest is one of the most reliable sources of energy you'll ever find.

Why Mental Energy Matters More Than Ever

When we stop learning, something in us begins to shrink.

Not physically, but spiritually.

But when we stay curious—when we say yes to wonder, when we let our brains be stretched in new directions—we feel alive again.

You don't need to memorize facts or master Shakespeare.

You just need to stay in the habit of wondering.

Asking questions.

Exploring possibilities.

Stretching your mind around something new—even something small.

That little flicker of discovery—that feeling of "oh, that's interesting"—is one of the surest signs that your spirit is still fully awake.

And here's the secret:

Staying mentally sharp isn't just about avoiding decline. It's about expanding what's possible for you now—so you can bring more of yourself into every moment.

Physical Energy: Motion Is Medicine

Let's talk about your body—not from a place of pressure, but from a place of potential.

There's a belief floating around that as we get older, we're supposed to slow down, shrink back, sit more, and move less.

But here's the truth:

You don't need six-pack abs. You need stamina.

You need the strength to say "yes" to the moments that matter:

- Walking with a friend and losing track of time

- Lifting your grandchild high into the air
- Dancing without hesitation at a wedding
- Gardening without soreness the next day
- Waking up and moving through your day without pain holding you back

You don't need a gym membership (unless you enjoy it).

You need a rhythm of movement that supports the life you want to live.

The question isn't: "What's my workout routine?"

It's: "How do I build a lifestyle that keeps me moving with joy?"

Here are a few approachable, energizing ways to start:

- Walk daily, even for just 10 minutes—especially outdoors, where nature adds its own boost
- Stretch in the morning, loosening the places that sleep has tightened
- Do something playful that raises your heart rate—a dance, a swim, a game of pickleball
- Stand tall, hydrate well, and breathe deeply—these small things recalibrate your system

Movement doesn't have to be intense.

But it does need to be intentional.

Because every step you take now is a vote for mobility later. And every moment of movement is a reminder: I'm still in this life. I still have energy to offer.

Retirement isn't the season to stop moving.

It's your opportunity to move more freely—because for once, your time is your own.

Make it count.

Not with pressure—but with presence.

Emotional Resilience: Don't Numb Out

Here's something we don't talk about enough:

Sometimes, the hardest part of retirement isn't what's missing from your schedule.
It's what's missing from your emotional landscape.

No more workplace tension. No daily stressors. No last-minute crises to solve.

Sounds peaceful, right?

But for many people, that kind of stillness can begin to feel like emotional drift.

There are no dramatic highs or lows. Just a long stretch of silence. And in that space, something sneaky can slip in:

Numbing.

You scroll.

You snack.

You fill your calendar with low-effort distractions.

You lose track of what you feel—because feeling nothing is easier than facing the discomfort of change.

But here's what's really happening:

That's your emotional life raising its hand, whispering: "Please don't forget about me."

Instead of numbing, try noticing.

Ask:

- Who do I talk to about things that really matter?
- What do I feel when I give myself time to slow down?
- Am I nourishing my inner life—or just avoiding it?

Emotional vitality doesn't come from having everything figured out.

It comes from being willing to feel.

The joy.

The grief.

The confusion.

The wonder.

When you give yourself permission to feel all of it, your life begins to feel real again.

And real is where the richness lives.

Spiritual Anchoring: Reconnecting with What Grounds You

Spiritual health isn't always about religion.

But it's always about meaning.

It's about the invisible thread that connects you to something beyond your own reflection.

It's the force that reminds you—you're not just a collection of tasks and memories.

You are a soul. A light. A story still unfolding.

And retirement, with all its space and silence, invites you to reconnect with that part of yourself.

For some, it's found in faith—through prayer, meditation, sacred text, or shared worship.

For others, it's felt in nature—in the rustle of leaves, the shape of clouds, the rhythm of waves.

It might emerge in creative expression—the slow dance of brush on canvas, pen on paper, hand on wood.

It may come through community service, through giving your time in quiet acts of compassion.

Or it might be found in stillness—in a quiet room, a morning sunrise, a deep breath that says, I'm here.

Your spirit is not a separate part of you.
It is the deepest part of you.
And when you feed it, everything else—your energy, your clarity, your joy—comes into alignment.

Spiritual anchoring doesn't require certainty.

It requires openness.

An openness to mystery. To connection. To meaning.

And to the profound realization that you're still becoming.

Energy Isn't Just a Gift—It's a Practice

Here's something I've come to believe with full conviction:

Energy isn't reserved for the young. It belongs to the engaged.

The most vibrant people I know in retirement aren't chasing youth.

They're chasing aliveness.

They've made peace with the fact that energy isn't something you're handed.

It's something you cultivate—with attention, with love, and with discipline.

They're people who:

- Say yes to what excites them
- Say no to what depletes them
- Move their bodies, even a little, every day
- Feed their minds with books, conversations, questions
- Tend to their emotional world—naming what's real

- Connect with their spirit through stillness, service, and awe
- And show up—fully, imperfectly, joyfully—for this remarkable chapter of life

Staying sharp doesn't mean being perfect.
It means staying in motion—not just physically, but mentally, emotionally, and spiritually.

It means choosing vitality over autopilot.

Presence over performance.

Joy over obligation.

So no, retirement doesn't mean stepping aside.

It means stepping in—deeper, more intentionally, more alive than ever before.

Coming Next: Planning for the Unexpected

Because even with good habits and sharp minds, life can still surprise us.

Health changes. Family needs arise. The unplanned knocks at the door.

But readiness isn't about control.

It's about knowing who you are and how to stay steady—even when life throws a curveball.

Let's talk about how to prepare—not out of fear, but with confidence.

Chapter 8
Planning for the Unexpected

Let's face it—no matter how thoughtfully you prepare, how neat your folders are, how updated your emergency contacts look, or how hopeful you feel heading into retirement…

Life still throws curveballs.

It doesn't ask for permission.

It doesn't follow your retirement calendar.

It doesn't care how many things you've checked off your to-do list.

One moment, you're flowing through retirement with confidence and rhythm.

You've found your groove. You know what days feel like now. You've even got a few plans booked and a new hobby you're enjoying.

Then—everything changes.

A sudden diagnosis.

A fall.

A financial loss.

A phone call that shakes your world.

Or maybe it's not something dramatic—maybe it's just a slow fade: a shift in energy, a creeping loneliness, a spouse's changing health.

And suddenly, the solid ground beneath your feet doesn't feel so steady.

The wind gets knocked out of your sails, and you realize— this wasn't in the plan.

And that's the hard part.

Because you did plan. You did prepare. You thought ahead.

You were told that if you got everything in order, retirement would unfold with ease and grace.

But here's the truth no one likes to say out loud:

Planning is essential—but it doesn't make you invincible.

And that's not a failure.

It's just… life.

No one likes to talk about this part of retirement. The unexpected. The unwanted. The unplanned.

But if we avoid it, we risk being caught off guard—not just practically, but emotionally. Spiritually. Relationally.

This chapter is not about dread.

It's not about bracing for disaster.

It's about building the kind of mindset and structure that lets you breathe through change instead of being buried by it.

It's about readiness, not rigidity.

Resilience, not resistance.

Because the question is never if life will surprise you.

The question is always:

"How will I respond when it does?"

The Illusion of Control

Let's start with something that may feel hard to admit, especially if you've been the one others relied on for years:

Many people walk into retirement with a quiet belief that they've finally earned control.

And to be fair, you have.

You can wake up when you want.

You can choose how your days look.

You can say no without guilt and yes without needing permission.

You've stepped off the treadmill. You've stopped sprinting.

Now, for the first time in decades, your time is your own.

That control feels empowering—and it should.

But it can also be misleading.

Because somewhere beneath that control is a hidden assumption:

"If I do all the right things, I can keep life from falling apart."

But here's what we all eventually come to understand:

Control is not the same as immunity.

You are not immune to:

- A loved one's illness
- Your own unexpected health issue
- Financial downturns
- Family tensions
- Emotional low points
- Grief that hits out of nowhere

And most importantly—you are not failing when life doesn't go according to plan.

You are not "doing retirement wrong" if you feel disoriented or afraid.

You are not "less wise" or "less prepared" because something painful caught you off guard.

You're simply human.

What retirement gives you—if you let it—is not insulation from change.

It's perspective in the face of it.

It offers the time to step back and reflect.

The margin to respond rather than react.

The wisdom to see what truly matters and the courage to let go of what doesn't.

Control is a myth. But clarity? That's real.
And clarity allows you to face the unpredictable with steadiness.

You've Been Here Before

Let's take a moment to remember something essential—something easy to forget when uncertainty creeps in:

You've done this before.

This isn't the first time life has caught you off guard.

It's not the first time a chapter changed before you were ready.

It's not the first time you stood at the edge of something unknown and wondered, What now?

Think back.

You've navigated change and challenge before:

- The move that uprooted your sense of place and made you start over
- The job loss or shift that forced you to rethink your purpose
- The diagnosis that changed your relationship with your body—and your sense of control
- The grief that felt like it might break you—and yet, in time, helped you grow in ways you never imagined

You've faced storms.
And you've found your footing, again and again.

Not because you had perfect answers.

But because you showed up anyway.

Because even in the face of fear or pain, you chose to keep moving forward.

You adapted. You learned. You softened and strengthened at the same time.

That wisdom? It didn't disappear with your job title.

It didn't fade when your routines changed.

It lives in you now—deeper, wiser, more available than ever before.

Retirement won't shield you from life's curveballs. But it gives you a gift:

More space to respond with intention.

More time to reflect.

More emotional margin.

More access to the kind of presence that turns fear into clarity and chaos into calm.

You are not a beginner in resilience.

You are already becoming the kind of person who weathers storms with grace.

When Life Changes Without Asking Permission

I once worked with a couple who retired within a month of each other. They were healthy, adventurous, and full of plans.

They had mapped out everything:

The road trips. The cruise. The new hiking trails. The time with grandkids.

They even had a vision board—literal cut-out pictures of their second act.

But just a couple of months into their freedom, everything changed.

She was diagnosed with a serious illness. The kind that stops you in your tracks.

Their calendar, once full of new adventures, filled with doctors' appointments, treatment plans, and tests.

And yet—what amazed me most wasn't the disruption. It was how they responded.

They didn't fall apart.

Yes, they cried. Yes, they were afraid. But there was something else.

They were clear. They were grounded. They were united.

They had already had the conversations that most people avoid:

- About what matters most
- About how they want to support each other

- About what it means to truly live, even when plans change

Because they'd talked about their values, they didn't scramble when life veered off course.

They adjusted—together.

And in that adjustment, they discovered something that became even more beautiful than their vision board:

The strength of shared clarity.

Anticipate, Don't Obsess

Let's be clear:

Planning for the unexpected doesn't mean bracing for doom.

It doesn't mean anxiously trying to control every possible outcome.

It means being willing to have honest conversations—now—so you're not scrambling later.

It means asking the questions that might feel uncomfortable, but ultimately build peace:

- What would I want if my health declined?
- Who do I trust to make decisions on my behalf?
- Do my loved ones know my wishes? Have we talked about it?
- If I became a caregiver, how would I care for myself in the process?
- How do I protect my emotional energy, without shutting down or burning out?

These questions don't bring fear.

They bring freedom.

Freedom from ambiguity.

Freedom from avoidable tension.

Freedom from having to make impossible decisions in the middle of emotional chaos.

They won't stop the hard moments.

But they will steady you when those moments arrive.

Resilience Isn't Built in Crisis

When life is going smoothly, it's easy to feel resilient.

But true resilience—the kind that lasts—isn't built in a crisis.

It's built before the storm.

It's cultivated in the choices you make now:

- Choosing to build relationships that offer more than surface-level comfort
- Choosing daily habits that strengthen your body and clear your mind
- Choosing spiritual grounding, whatever that looks like for you
- Choosing purpose over passivity
- Choosing clarity over avoidance

Resilience isn't about gritting your teeth.
It's about preparing the soil—so that when the storm comes, your roots hold firm.

Ask yourself:

- What anchors me when everything else is uncertain?

- What helps me return to myself, even when I'm hurting?
- What do I want to lean on—not just when things are easy, but when they're hard?

That's the kind of preparation that leads to peace, not panic.

Build a Support Plan Before You Need It

Here's a truth we often resist:

You don't have to do this alone.
In fact, you shouldn't.

When life shifts unexpectedly, the most helpful thing isn't a perfect plan.

It's a strong support system.

So take time—right now, while things are calm—to build your support network with intention.

- Know your inner circle. Who can you call at 2 a.m. if things go sideways? Who really shows up for you?

- Identify professionals you trust. Doctors, financial advisors, legal experts—do you have their info handy?
- Open the hard conversations with family. Don't assume they know your wishes. Create the space to talk openly.
- Keep key documents accessible. Healthcare directives, contact lists, preferences—make sure they're easy to find.
- Write down your priorities. What do you want people to remember about how you handled this time in your life?

This isn't about morbid scenarios.

It's about love in action.

It's about making life easier for your future self—and for the people who love you most.

That's not pessimism.
That's leadership.

And leadership, especially in this chapter, often looks like quiet courage, wise planning, and radical clarity.

Emotional Flexibility Matters

When life shifts unexpectedly, the first thing many people reach for is a plan.

And yes—logistics matter.

Clear instructions. Legal documents. Practical checklists.

But when the ground really shakes, it's not the paperwork that holds you steady.

It's your emotional flexibility.

It's your ability to stretch instead of snap.

To feel the full weight of change—and still breathe through it.

To grieve what's been lost while still believing in what can grow.

Ask yourself:

- Can I hold space for grief without being defined by it?
- Can I adjust my path without losing my identity?
- Can I discover new meaning—even when my old vision has crumbled?

These aren't easy questions. But they are essential ones.

Because emotional flexibility is not about staying positive.

It's not about pushing down discomfort or pretending to be okay when you're not.

It's about staying open—to change, to emotion, to transformation.

It's the ability to say:

- "This hurts... and I can keep going."
- "This wasn't the plan... and I can still live well."
- "This isn't what I expected... but something new might still emerge."

The people who navigate life's hardest seasons with grace aren't the ones who escape pain.

They're the ones who allow space for it—without letting it define their entire story.

They honor their tears, their fears, their uncertainty.

And they keep showing up—open to whatever beauty might still rise from the ashes.

Retirement Isn't a Bubble—It's Life, Continued

There's a cultural myth that retirement is a gentle fade into quiet.

That it's the final exhale after decades of effort.

That life gets simpler, smaller, softer.

And in some ways, that's true.

You do step away from the grind.

You do get more time for rest and reflection.

But let's be clear:

Retirement isn't a retreat from life. It is life.

And life—at every stage—is beautifully complex.

It's joy and sorrow.

Laughter and loss.

Control and surrender.

Certainty and surprise.

It's learning how to be fully present in this moment, even when you can't predict the next.

You don't get to opt out of the hard things now.

But you do get to bring all the wisdom you've earned into how you face them.

You get to respond with a steadier voice.

You get to choose presence over panic.

You get to hold your values close and your loved ones closer.

This chapter isn't about building walls to keep the world out.

It's about planting roots so you can stay grounded no matter what the world brings in.

Roots in your relationships.

Roots in your health.

Roots in your purpose.

Roots in your faith, your integrity, your inner knowing.

Because when your roots run deep, you don't fear the storm. You trust your foundation.

Here's the invitation:

Don't wait for crisis to learn how to bend.

Start now.

Start with reflection.

Start by building your emotional strength—not through toughness, but through tenderness.

Because this life will surprise you.

But it can also shape you in the most unexpected and beautiful ways.

And the more open you are to that shaping, the more resilient—and radiant—your retirement will become.

Coming Next: Reimagining Work in Retirement

If legacy is about how we live and what we leave behind, then work—how we contribute our time, talents, and energy—plays a powerful role in shaping that legacy.

But here's the good news:

In retirement, work doesn't have to look anything like it used to.

Gone are the days of job titles, annual reviews, and the 9-to-5 grind.

What remains is something more open, more flexible, and more personal.

Now, you get to redefine what work means—on your terms.

It could be:

- A new chapter of meaningful service
- A part-time role that lights you up
- A creative project you've postponed for years
- Mentoring someone walking a path you know well
- Or simply showing up with presence in ways that make a difference

Work in this season isn't about achievement.

It's about alignment—connecting what you do with who you are and how you want to give.

If you've ever said, "I don't want to stop working—but I want to do work that matters," this next chapter is for you.

Let's explore what it looks like to reimagine work in retirement—not as obligation, but as opportunity.

Chapter 9
Reimagining Work in Retirement

There's a persistent myth floating around, often whispered between retirement parties and echoed in glossy brochures:

"Retirement means the end of work."

You leave the office.

You turn in the keys, the name badge, the laptop.

You mark the calendar with one final circle and say, "I'm done."

And in many ways—you are.

You've shown up for decades.

You've met the deadlines, led the meetings, solved the problems.

You've earned your rest. Truly.

But here's the secret many discover just a few months in:

Retirement doesn't mark the end of work.
It marks the beginning of working differently.

Because for those of us wired to create… to guide… to serve… to lead— the impulse to contribute doesn't retire just because we do.

The drive to be part of something bigger than ourselves doesn't dissolve the moment we hand in a keycard.

It shifts. It softens.

But it stays.

Work Doesn't Disappear—It Evolves

Work doesn't disappear after retirement.

What changes is your relationship with it.

In your previous chapters, work might have been about:
- Security
- Status
- Providing for a family
- Climbing a ladder
- Meeting expectations
- Proving your worth

But now?

Now, you're not working to survive.
You're working to mean something.

You're showing up not for performance—but for purpose.

Not because someone else is counting on you—but because you want to count on yourself.

This is work born of freedom.

Work that aligns with your values, not your resume.

Work that flows from the heart, not from the pressure of quarterly reports.

You're no longer bound by outcomes.

You're invited into impact.

Work Isn't the Enemy—Burnout Is

Let's get honest for a moment.

What we were often desperate to escape when we envisioned retirement…

Wasn't the work.

It was the grind.

The endless meetings that drained you.

The inbox that never stayed empty.

The performance reviews that focused more on numbers than people.

The exhausting pace that left no room for breath—let alone joy.

That kind of working? Yes, it needed to end.

But now that you've stepped away from the hustle, you may notice something surprising creeping back in:

- A sense of restlessness
- A quiet longing to be useful
- The itch to solve a problem or guide someone through theirs
- The desire to build, serve, create, or contribute—without burning out this time

What we're really retiring from is burnout—not purpose.

And here lies the invitation of this chapter:

To rediscover the parts of work you loved—without the parts that depleted you.

To contribute without collapsing.

To give without being emptied.

To offer your wisdom, experience, or creativity—on your own terms, in your own rhythm, and with joy at the center.

Because work is not the enemy.

Exhaustion is.

An Encore—Not an Exit

You don't need to "go back."

You don't need to fill your calendar with busywork or prove your value through productivity.

But for many, the most fulfilling path forward is not to exit the stage entirely—

It's to step back in for an encore.

A second act.

A new expression of old gifts.

A way to work not because you have to, but because you want to.

Encore work often looks like:

- Consulting or mentoring in your area of experience
- Launching a small side business or nonprofit
- Teaching, coaching, or supporting causes you care about
- Turning a long-held passion into a project with purpose
- Volunteering in a way that lights you up, not just fills time

The key? It's work on your terms.

Flexible. Fulfilling.

Rooted in joy—not driven by pressure.

You're not done working.
You're just ready to work in a way that feels deeply alive.

The Rise of the Encore Career

Something beautiful is happening across the retirement landscape.

More and more people are stepping out of their traditional careers—not to stop working altogether, but to start working differently.

It's not a retreat.
It's a reinvention.

This movement has a name: the encore career.

It's not about climbing a new ladder.

It's about taking your years of experience, your hard-won wisdom, your natural gifts—and using them in a way that feels purposeful, energizing, and freeing.

You're not chasing achievement anymore.

You're chasing alignment.

What Does an Encore Career Look Like?

An encore career doesn't have a single path.

It's as unique as you are.

It might look like:

- Consulting in your field—but on your terms, without the old politics or pressure
- Mentoring someone younger who's navigating a road you've already walked
- Launching a nonprofit that solves a local problem you've cared about for years
- Starting a business from a passion that never had room to grow
- Teaching or coaching, formally or informally, in a space that lights you up
- Turning a hobby—woodworking, gardening, baking, painting—into a creative outlet or small income stream

Some people step into these encore roles full-time.

Others give just a few hours a week.

The common thread?

It's work that feels aligned, not assigned.
It's contribution born from freedom—not pressure.

You're not here to prove yourself anymore.

You're here to be yourself—and let that be enough.

In this stage of life, work becomes a vehicle not for success, but for significance.

A Story: The Consultant Who Brought His Wisdom Home

I knew a man who had spent over four decades in city planning.

He was one of those people who carried wisdom in the way he walked into a room—never loud, never flashy, but always grounded and thoughtful.

He made people better simply by listening to them well.

When he retired, he thought he'd take a year to rest. Sleep in. Travel. Catch up on books and house projects. But three months in, he started feeling… off.

"I thought I'd feel free," he told me. "But I felt unmoored. Like I was floating without purpose."

His wife, who knew him well, gently said one afternoon,

"You've still got too much in you to sit still for long."

And she was right.

So, he started small.

He began volunteering with a neighborhood association, offering advice on traffic flow and zoning. Nothing intense. Just conversations. Just showing up.

Before long, word spread.

A few rural towns reached out, asking for help thinking through their growth plans.

He began consulting part-time—on his terms. No office. No suit. No long hours. Just purpose.

"It's the best kind of work," he said.
"I don't need to be in charge. I just get to offer what I know— and leave at the end of the day knowing I made something better."

That's what encore work can look like.

No pressure.

Just presence.

Just purpose.

Just enough.

What's In Your Work DNA?

One of the most powerful questions you can ask in retirement is this:

"What's in my work DNA?"

Not your job title.

Not your resume.

But your natural way of contributing—the ways you've always added value, solved problems, or helped others thrive.

Take a few minutes to reflect:

- What kind of work has always lit me up, regardless of pay or recognition?
- What activities or roles made me lose track of time?
- Who could benefit from my experience, presence, or insight right now?
- What's something I've always wanted to do—but didn't have time or permission to explore before?
- If I could design my work-life from scratch—what would it look like?
- What boundaries would I put in place to protect my peace, energy, and joy?

You don't need a five-year plan.

You don't need to build a business empire or write a 50-page proposal.

You just need honest questions—and the courage to follow where they lead.

Sometimes the answer will feel bold and exciting.

Sometimes it'll be quiet and tender.

But in every case, meaningful work begins with meaningful reflection.

Encore Isn't About Ambition—It's About Alignment

If your encore path includes income, that's fine.

But many retirees choose these new roles not because they need the money—but because they want the mission.

They want to:
- Keep growing
- Stay engaged
- Help others
- Create beauty
- Lead with wisdom
- Feel the rhythm of contribution without the cost of burnout

This isn't about proving you've still "got it."

This is about giving what you've always had—but now in a way that brings life back to you, too.

Redefining Productivity

Let's take a moment to reclaim a word that's often been twisted by years of deadlines, deliverables, and performance reviews:

Productivity.

For decades, productivity may have meant checking off to-do lists, replying to emails at all hours, keeping plates spinning while trying not to let anything drop.

But in this next chapter, productivity deserves a new definition.

Not busyness.

Not burnout.

Not filling your time so you don't feel useless.

In this season, productivity means fruitfulness.

It means tending to what matters—not what simply keeps you occupied.

It's not about staying busy so you don't feel bored.

It's about being intentional so you feel alive.

Ask yourself:

- What makes me feel awake, curious, or energized?
- What kinds of effort leave me feeling fulfilled, not just exhausted?
- What do I want to look back on and say, "That was time well spent"?

For some, that answer might be:

- Mentoring one person each month
- Leading a service project that brings neighbors together
- Recording stories for future generations
- Writing a blog or starting a podcast that shares your hard-earned insights
- Spending time with someone who's lonely and just needs to be seen

- Creating beauty—through gardening, painting, building, baking, music

Whatever it is, the metric is different now.

It's not about checking the box.
It's about checking in—with your heart.

What brings you joy when the day ends?

What makes you feel like you added something meaningful to the world?

That's your new productivity.

And the most beautiful part?

You're not doing it for a paycheck.
You're doing it because this is the kind of life you want to live.

You Get to Choose

There's something deeply empowering about this stage of life:

You don't have to. You get to.

You're no longer working from fear—of losing your job, missing a bonus, or falling behind.

You're not climbing a ladder or defending a reputation.

You've already proven yourself.

Now, you get to respond to what calls you, not what controls you.

You get to:
- Say yes to what excites you
- Say no to what drains you
- Say not now to anything that doesn't align with your energy or priorities

You get to live and work from a place of freedom—not obligation.

Let that freedom guide your next step.

Ask yourself:

- What am I genuinely excited to say yes to?
- What rhythms help protect my peace and renew my energy?
- What kind of impact do I want to leave behind—not someday, but starting today?

Because here's the truth:

You don't have to leave a legacy in capital letters.

You just must live with intention today.

One choice at a time.

One conversation at a time.

One generous, grounded "yes" at a time.

This isn't about proving your worth.
It's about pouring out your heart in ways that feel right, true, and meaningful.

That choice—to shape your days around what matters most to you?

That changes everything.

Chapter 10
Creativity in the Second Act

Let me say something that might surprise you—

Especially if your life has been more practical than poetic,

More checklists than canvas,

More meetings than melodies:

You are a creative person.

Yes, you.

Even if you've never painted a landscape.

Even if your handwriting never looked like calligraphy.

Even if your job was about spreadsheets, strategy, or raising a family more than sketching, sculpting, or songwriting.

Because creativity isn't about being artistic.
It's about being alive.

It's about curiosity.

It's about wonder.

It's about using your energy to bring something into the world that wasn't there before.

That "something" might be:

- A story that needed to be told
- A table set with care for friends
- A rearranged room that reflects your spirit
- A garden that welcomes butterflies and grandchildren alike
- A quiet journal filled with thoughts you've never shared

Creativity is the way your soul whispers, "I'm still here. I still want to make something."

And in retirement?

Creativity is not an add-on.
It's a lifeline—to joy, to purpose, and to vitality.

The Gift of Creative Space

For decades, your schedule was full.

You were needed.

You were busy.

You had people to care for, tasks to complete, deadlines to meet.

In between all of that, you may have had fleeting moments where inspiration stirred—a desire to write, to paint, to play.

But then dinner needed to be made.

Or the inbox dinged.

Or someone else's needs came first.

And so, you said, "Someday."

But here you are.

Welcome to someday.

Retirement has given you something most people only dream about:

Space.

Space to breathe.

Space to listen inward.

Space to pick up something new—or rediscover something old.

You don't need to monetize your creativity.

You don't need to be good at it.

You don't need a platform or a plan.

You just need to ask:

"What would I love to create—not for recognition, but for joy?"

And then—begin.

Begin slowly.

Begin awkwardly.

Begin with permission to make something beautifully imperfect.

Because the goal is not perfection.

The goal is presence.

Reclaiming Lost Passions

I've spoken with so many retirees who have said the same sentence, almost word for word:

"I used to love ___… but I haven't done it in years."

And when they fill in the blank—piano, painting, pottery, puzzles, poetry—something shifts.

Their eyes light up.

Their voice softens.

There's a flicker of something sacred rising to the surface.

It's not nostalgia.
It's memory waking up a piece of identity that's been quietly waiting.

Life, with all its busyness and beauty, has a way of burying our passions beneath its responsibilities.

But just because something has been silent doesn't mean it has disappeared.

It's still there.

Waiting.

Patiently.

Lovingly.

Waiting for your permission to come back.

Maybe for you it was:

- Strumming your guitar on quiet evenings
- Writing short stories in the back of a notebook
- Baking sourdough bread by feel, not recipe
- Sketching in parks and on napkins at cafes
- Making stained glass, candles, birdhouses
- Designing flower beds that were more art than landscaping
- Dancing when no one was watching

Whatever it was, it belonged to you.
And it still does.

That passion hasn't left you.

It's been tucked away—beneath the meetings, the caregiving, the deadlines, the obligations.

And now?

Now is the moment to say:

"Let's try again."

It's Not About Mastery. It's About Joy.

One woman told me a story I'll never forget.

She said,

"I started painting again—not to sell it, not to frame it, not to prove anything. I just wanted to see what would happen. And what happened was... I came back to life."

That's the gift of reclaimed creativity.

It doesn't just make things.

It remakes us.

It gives us a chance to meet ourselves again—not the productive self or the responsible self, but the imaginative, playful, wonder-filled part that often gets lost in adulthood.

And here's the most beautiful part:

That part of you is still intact.
All it needs is a little attention—and a little space.

A Story: The Gardener Who Found His Voice

I once met a man who had spent 40 years in logistics.

Smart. Reliable. Quiet.

He knew how to solve problems, manage systems, keep things running smoothly.

You probably wouldn't have called him "creative."

He certainly didn't call himself that.

But after he retired, he decided to plant a tomato garden. Just a few rows. Just to stay active. Just to do something with his hands.

Then came basil. Then came roses. Then came lavender and lemon balm.

Pretty soon, he was waking up at 6:30 a.m.—not because he had to, but because he couldn't wait to walk outside and see what had bloomed overnight.

"It feels like I'm collaborating with nature," he told me. "I do my part. It does its part. And together, we create something beautiful."

That garden became his voice.

His therapy. His worship. His poetry.

He didn't need an audience.

He didn't need results.

He just needed a rhythm that allowed his soul to speak again.

And that's what creativity does.

It speaks not at us, but through us.
It's not a performance. It's a process.

The Science of Creativity and Aging

This isn't just romantic.

It's remarkably practical.

Research on aging and creativity is clear and compelling:

Engaging in creative activity has been shown to:

- Boost mood and reduce symptoms of anxiety and depression
- Improve memory and cognitive flexibility
- Regulate emotions, especially during periods of transition or loss
- Enhance resilience, self-esteem, and overall well-being
- Foster a renewed sense of identity and purpose
- Even help reduce the risk of cognitive decline

And here's the best news:
Creativity doesn't fade with age. It deepens.

Because you've seen more.

You've felt more.

You've lived through more.

And all of that becomes rich material for creative expression.

Whether you're writing, gardening, crafting, singing, building, or simply wondering—your creativity now is informed by a lifetime of perspective.

You don't need to be prolific.

You don't need to be polished.

You just need to begin.

It Doesn't Have to Be Art

Maybe "creative" still doesn't feel like a word that fits you.

Maybe you've always thought of creativity as something other people have—musicians, artists, writers, designers.

But let me tell you something I believe deeply:

Creativity is not a profession. It's a posture.

It's not about galleries or awards.

It's about how you bring your energy, attention, and imagination into everyday life.

You are being creative when you:

- Design a meaningful experience—a dinner, a celebration, a ritual
- Write your family's story, even if it's just for your grandkids
- Invent a new recipe, blending flavors from your past with what you have on hand
- Build something from wood, from words, from nothing
- Record your voice, passing on stories, jokes, memories, songs
- Rearrange your living space in a way that feels like the new you
- Start a storytelling group or discussion circle at the library or over Zoom

The medium doesn't matter.
The engagement does.

Creativity is what happens when your soul reaches for expression—through cooking, crafting, connecting, or caring.

It lives not just in what you make, but in how you make meaning.

Creativity as a Spiritual Practice

There's something sacred about creating.

It doesn't have to look religious to be spiritual.

Because when you make something—when you slow down, listen inward, follow a thread of curiosity—you are doing more than creating a product.

You are coming home to yourself.

Creativity:
- Slows the noise of the outside world
- Softens your breath and sharpens your focus
- Anchors you in the present moment, fully alive, fully human

And it reminds you:

You are not just a consumer of life.
You are a participant in it.

You don't need credentials.

You don't need anyone's permission.

You don't need to be "good" at it.

You just need to be:

- Open to curiosity
- Available to wonder
- Willing to be surprised

Sometimes creativity shows up in:

- A quilt stitched slowly over weeks
- A watercolor that captures how you feel without words
- A poem written in the margins of a journal
- A quiet Saturday spent rearranging your books, lighting a candle, and making space for reflection

You are still becoming.

And creativity is how you meet the parts of yourself that haven't arrived yet.

Start Where You Are

Not sure where to begin?

Good. That means you're exactly where you need to be.

Try this simple practice:

1. List five things you enjoyed doing as a kid or young adult—before life got busy.
2. Circle one that still stirs a little curiosity or joy.
3. Give it one hour this week. Just one. No strings attached.
4. Let go of results. Let go of needing to be good. Let go of judgment.
5. Just show up and play.

You don't need a goal.

You need a little permission.

Don't aim to be productive.

Don't aim to be impressive.

Aim to be present.

Because something always stirs when we create—not just a finished product, but a long-forgotten part of ourselves.

It doesn't just awaken your hands.
It awakens your heart.

A Life That Feels Alive

Creativity doesn't just add color to your calendar.

It adds texture to your soul.

It gives shape to your feelings.

It gives space to your longings.

It gives voice to what your heart has been quietly trying to say.

In a world that often reduces worth to productivity or titles, creativity whispers a deeper truth:

"You are worthy simply because you are alive—and you still have something to express."

So pick up the pen.

Pick up the camera.

Pick up the brush.

Pick up the spoon, the saw, the fabric, the tool.

Pick up whatever is calling your name.

Make something.

Not to impress.

But to be honest.

Not for an audience.

But for yourself.

Because when you create, you don't just make art or objects or meals or spaces.

You make meaning.
You make connection.
You make a more joyful, grounded version of yourself.

And in doing so, you remind the world—and yourself—that the second act of life can be not only productive, but beautifully expressive.

Coming Next: A Retirement Built on Gratitude

Because once you begin seeing yourself as a creator, you begin noticing more beauty.

And noticing more beauty? That's the first step toward living a life rooted in thankfulness.

Let's explore that next.

Chapter 11
A Retirement Built on Gratitude

Let me ask you something simple—but not always easy:

What are you grateful for today?

Not in general.

Not what you think you should be thankful for.

Not a generic list of blessings.

But right now—in this breath, in this moment—

What makes your shoulders relax?

What softens your chest or slows your thoughts?

What quietly reminds you, "This... this is enough"?

Sometimes gratitude doesn't roar.

It whispers.

It arrives not in life's big celebrations, but in the softest pauses:

- The smell of fresh coffee drifting through the kitchen
- The golden glow of sunlight across the counter
- A friend who calls just because
- The gentle ache in your muscles after a walk
- The peace of knowing you don't have to rush

These are not small things.

They're sacred.

Because the truth is, gratitude doesn't always come with confetti.

It comes with clarity. With stillness. With the courage to notice the ordinary.

And this chapter—this whole chapter—is about building your second act not on striving, but on seeing.

Not on acquiring, but on appreciating.

Because few things transform a life more than learning to recognize when you already have enough.

Gratitude Isn't Just Politeness—It's Perspective

Let's be honest—there's a lot of confusion about what gratitude actually is.

Some think it means plastering on a smile when you feel like falling apart.

Some think it's about being cheerful no matter what.

Some turn it into a performance—"Just be grateful!" they say, as if that should cancel your pain.

But that's not real gratitude.

That's bypassing.

True gratitude doesn't deny what's hard.

It doesn't diminish your grief or mask your disappointment.

Gratitude is deeper. Wiser. More honest.

It's not about pretending everything is fine.

It's about pausing long enough to see that not everything is broken.

It's a quiet but courageous act of perspective.

It says:

"Yes, this part of life is hard.
And yet—this part is still beautiful."

Gratitude doesn't erase your sadness.

It makes room for it—and surrounds it with enough light to help you keep going.

It expands your story beyond the struggle.

It helps you notice what you still have.

Not because everything is perfect.
But because you've chosen to see what's still true, still good, still worth holding close.

A Story: The Man with the Cane

I once met a man in his 70s who walked with a cane after major surgery.

He said,

"I used to grumble about it every day. It felt like a constant reminder of what I'd lost."

But one morning, something shifted.

He looked at the cane and whispered to it,

"You let me walk."

That small change in perspective changed everything.

He didn't suddenly like the cane.

But he began to appreciate what it allowed.

"Gratitude gave me back my dignity," he told me. "I stopped seeing what I'd lost—and started seeing what I still had."

That's the quiet power of perspective.

It won't erase your pain.

But it will widen your view.

Why Gratitude Matters More in Retirement

Here's something no one tells you about retirement until you're living it:

When you walk away from your career, you're not just walking away from a job.
You're walking away from the daily affirmations that told you, "You matter."

You're no longer receiving:

- Performance reviews that validate your contributions
- Promotions that acknowledge your progress
- Feedback from colleagues that remind you you're needed
- Even the rhythm of being in demand, being asked, being seen

And while that can be incredibly freeing—it can also leave a hollow space.

A quiet absence of affirmation.

A silence that, over time, can feel less like peace and more like uncertainty.

You've gained time—but maybe lost a bit of clarity.

That's where gratitude steps in—not as a vague nicety, but as a new compass.

Because in retirement, the question shifts.

It's no longer:

"What did I achieve today?"
"What did I produce?"
"Who needed me?"

Instead, the more life-giving question becomes:

"What did I notice?"
"What did I receive?"
"What did I savor, offer, or honor?"

One line of questioning leads to pressure, performance, and potential burnout—just like before.

But the other?

It opens the door to peace.

To reflection.
To a deeper connection with yourself and the present moment.

Gratitude becomes a spiritual practice.

A way of measuring not how much you did, but how fully you lived.

It becomes your way of anchoring joy—not in outcomes, but in awareness.

Practicing Gratitude: 5 Simple Tools

You don't need to be a journaler.

You don't need a fancy app or a perfectly curated morning routine.

You just need a little willingness.

Willingness to pause.

To look.

To notice what's already good—and to say thank you.

Here are five simple ways to begin (or deepen) your gratitude practice:

1. The Morning List

Before you reach for your phone or read the news, pause.

Write down three things you're grateful for—big or small.

- A good night's sleep
- The scent of toast
- A memory that still makes you smile
- A body that can still move, even if slower

Don't overthink it. Just begin.

You're training your mind to see goodness first.

2. The Daily Thank You

Tell one person each day—either out loud or silently—why you appreciate them.

It could be:

- A spouse who always puts on the coffee
- A neighbor who waves from their porch
- A store clerk who greets you by name
- A friend who once said something that stuck with you

Gratitude shared becomes connection deepened.

3. The Gratitude Walk

Step outside with no goal other than to notice five things you're grateful for before returning.

It might be:

- A breeze against your skin
- Flowers pushing up through the sidewalk crack
- A dog wagging its tail
- The sound of birds
- The feeling of being unhurried

Let the walk become a moving meditation.

Let the world remind you that goodness is everywhere.

4. The What-If Flip

The next time something annoys you—technology, traffic, noisy neighbors—try this:

Ask:

"What if I lost this tomorrow?"

It doesn't excuse the frustration, but it shifts your frame.

- The noisy house means there's still life around you
- The hard-to-open jar means you still have strength to try
- The mess in the living room means you've had people close

It's a fast, powerful reset from irritation to appreciation.

5. The Gratitude Letter

Once a month, write a short note or email to someone who's impacted your life.

It could be a teacher, a mentor, a childhood friend, or even someone you never properly thanked.

Don't wait for the "right" moment.

Just say thank you—no strings attached.

This one simple act often creates a ripple far beyond what you can see.

Each of these practices says, in its own quiet way:

"I choose to see what's still good."
"I choose to notice."
"I choose to live this chapter fully awake."

Because when you anchor your retirement in gratitude, it's no longer just a phase of life.

It becomes a practice of seeing.
A daily declaration: "This is enough. And I am, too."

Gratitude as a Legacy

Let's talk about legacy—not just what you leave behind, but how you live now in a way that lingers long after you're gone.

Because one of the most powerful things you can pass on isn't money, a trust, or even wisdom wrapped in words.

It's a way of seeing.

Imagine your grandchildren or nieces and nephews remembering you like this:

- As the one who always paused to admire a sunset
- Who noticed the bluebird on the fence or the steam rising off your coffee cup
- Who gave thanks out loud, not because it was polite, but because it was sincere
- Who laughed easily, listened fully, and cried when the moment called for it

Not performative gratitude, but embodied gratitude.

A way of walking through the world that says:

"Life is precious. Pay attention. Be kind. Say thank you."

That kind of presence teaches more than any lecture ever could.

It says, "This is how you live well. This is what matters."

That is a legacy of soul. And it will outlast almost anything else you build.

Even in Loss, There Is Thanks

We can't talk about gratitude without naming the full truth:

Gratitude doesn't cancel grief.

It doesn't erase the ache of what's been lost or fix the pain of what never came.

But it can walk beside it.

Some of the most deeply grateful people I know are also the ones who've walked through profound loss—of a spouse, a child, a dream, a life chapter.

And here's what they've taught me:

- Gratitude doesn't come instead of grief.
- It comes alongside it.
- It holds grief's hand.

When something sacred is taken, what remains becomes sacred too.

The coffee mug on the shelf.

The sound of the wind in the trees.

The photograph that now means even more than it did before.

The quiet act of being able to breathe, to move, to cry, to notice.

Gratitude doesn't always sparkle.

Sometimes it arrives through tears.

Sometimes it's just a whisper.

But even then—it shines.
And when you allow it in, even gently, it becomes a thread of light in the darker moments.

Let Gratitude Shape the Way Forward

You don't have to fake it.

You don't have to force it.

You don't need to wait for a mountaintop moment to begin.

You just need to start where you are.

Look up.
Look around.
Look within.

And ask:

"What in this moment is worth noticing?"

Because when you develop the habit of seeing—of truly noticing what's already here—you begin to live a different kind of life.

Not one marked by what you lack, but by what you have.

Not a life that's winding down—but one that's waking up.

In that posture, everything changes.

You begin to live with intention.

With tenderness.

With awe.

You begin to see retirement not as the end of something—but the blossoming of everything that's been waiting beneath the surface.

Closing Reflection

"Gratitude turns what we have into enough—
And enough into abundance."
– Anonymous

So I'll ask again:

What are you thankful for today?

Write it down.

Say it out loud.

Let it soften your spirit. Let it redirect your energy. Let it become your next quiet step toward joy.

Because joy doesn't always come wrapped in confetti.

Sometimes it enters quietly—

Carried in the arms of gratitude.

Coming Next: Living Your Legacy

Because no matter what happens next—through the highs and lows, the planned and unplanned—the most powerful part of your retirement isn't what you accumulate.

It's what you leave behind.

Not just in your will.

But in your words.

Your actions.

Your values.

Your presence.

Let's explore how to make that legacy intentional—and unforgettable.

Chapter 12
Living Your Legacy

Let's pause here—right in the middle of your journey—and ask a question most people don't consider until the very end:

"What do I want to leave behind—not someday, but starting now?"

Most of us associate the word legacy with funerals, foundations, or final chapters. It's easy to think of legacy as something people summarize once you're gone—your accomplishments, your assets, the things that outlast you.

But legacy isn't just about the end of life.

It's about the shape your life takes right now.

It's not just about what you'll leave after you're gone.

It's about what you're leaving today—with your words, your presence, your energy, your love.

Legacy isn't something you archive. It's something you live.

Legacy Is Not a Monument—It's a Trail

Some people imagine legacy in grand, concrete terms:

- A building with their name on it
- A scholarship fund for future generations
- A large estate passed on in their will

And let's be clear—those things can be meaningful. They can change lives. They can be beautiful reflections of a life well lived.

But for most of us, legacy looks a little quieter.

Legacy is not a monument. It's a trail.

A trail made of footprints you didn't even realize you were leaving:

- The way your grandchild remembers how you knelt down, looked them in the eyes, and really listened

- The old colleague who still hears your voice when making a tough call
- The neighbor who was quietly watching how you handled adversity—and learned from it
- The friend who found courage in your honesty
- The volunteer who felt seen and valued because you took the time to say, "Thank you. You matter."

You don't leave that kind of legacy all at once.

You leave it one small, intentional moment at a time.

In every interaction, you are either reinforcing the story you want to live—or drifting from it.

So ask yourself:

- What am I planting in people's hearts?
- What do others feel when they're around me?
- What am I modeling—not with perfection, but with presence?

That's where legacy lives.

You're Still Leaving One—Whether You Mean To or Not

Here's something we don't often admit:

You're already creating a legacy—whether you're aware of it or not.

Every word you speak.

Every boundary you uphold.

Every moment of compassion or carelessness.

Every story you share—or choose not to.

It all leaves a mark.

So the real question isn't "Will I leave a legacy?"

The real question is:

"Am I living in a way that reflects the legacy I want to leave?"

Because there's tremendous power in this season of life.

You're no longer defined by the urgent demands of work or the expectations of others.

You have space now—precious space—to become more intentional with your time, your words, and your presence.

This chapter gives you the opportunity to align your life with your values.

To shift from doing to becoming.

From pressure to purpose.

And that alignment? That clarity?

That's where legacy shines its brightest.

Legacy Isn't About Being Remembered. It's About Being Real.

Some people fear that legacy is about being impressive—something to be preserved in headlines or history books.

But I've found that the most meaningful legacies don't come from trying to be important.

They come from choosing to be authentic.

They come from presence, not performance.

Your legacy lives in how you:

- Greet your neighbor
- Respond to setbacks
- Comfort someone who's hurting
- Celebrate someone else's joy
- Apologize when you're wrong
- Live your values when no one's watching

And most of all—your legacy is shaped by how fully you show up in the life you're still living.

A Legacy You Can Live Today

So don't wait.

Don't wait for your name to appear in someone's program or for a eulogy to summarize who you were.

Start now.

Start by asking:

- What do I want people to feel when they leave a conversation with me?
- What story do I want my family to tell—not about my achievements, but about my heart?
- What part of myself do I want to pass on, not just through possessions, but through love?

Maybe you write letters to your grandchildren.

Maybe you mentor a younger neighbor.

Maybe you record stories from your life—not because they're perfect, but because they're true.

Maybe you simply decide to speak more love, more kindness, more truth—starting today.

Legacy isn't a final act.

It's an everyday intention.

What Does a Legacy Life Look Like?

Let's take legacy out of the clouds and bring it back to the ground.

Because living your legacy doesn't require a spotlight. It doesn't depend on money, status, or a public platform.

A legacy life is one lived with intention—and it's almost always quieter than we imagine.

Legacy is built in the way you:

- Keep your word, even when it's inconvenient
- Apologize sincerely when you miss the mark
- Ask thoughtful questions, not just give answers
- Laugh freely and often
- Serve without needing recognition
- Choose joy, even in the midst of uncertainty

It's how you show up when you're tired.

How you treat the barista.

How you listen when someone's voice trembles.

How you treat people who can't offer you anything in return.

Your legacy is revealed not in one grand gesture—but in a thousand small, unnoticed choices.

It's how you love, how you lead, and how you live when no one is watching.

And the most powerful part?

You don't need to wait for a special moment to start.

You're already living it.

Every day.

Every interaction.

Every intention.

A Legacy Exercise: The "Three Words" Reflection

Here's a simple practice that can reveal a lot:

Find five quiet minutes.

Breathe deeply.

Set aside the to-do list and the expectations.

Then ask yourself:

"When the people who know me best describe me, what three words do I want them to use?"

Take your time.

Write them down.

Let them be true.

Let them reflect your heart—not what you think people want, but who you actually hope to become.

Now, take it one step further:

- Am I living those words—today?
- What small shifts could I make to embody them more consistently?

You might find that your answers point not to some distant aspiration, but to changes that begin with simple acts:

- A more patient response
- A more generous gesture
- A more courageous truth

Legacy, after all, begins in the present moment.

Not in a speech someone gives when you're gone, but in the way you move through the world—today.

Sharing Your Story Matters

If there's one powerful truth I hope you hold onto in this season, it's this:

Your story matters.

Not just the highlights.

Not just the successes.

Not just the parts that look good from the outside.

All of it.

What you got wrong.

What you learned the hard way.

What cracked you open and slowly pieced you back together.

Because somewhere, someone is walking a road you've already walked.

And your story—your courage to speak it—might just be the map they're looking for.

You don't have to be an author.

You don't have to publish a memoir.

Just speak your truth.

- Around a dinner table
- In a letter to your kids or grandkids
- At a storytelling night, a support group, a porch gathering
- Or quietly, as a mentor over coffee with someone younger who's still figuring it all out

Stories connect generations.
They heal shame. They pass on wisdom. They remind others that they're not alone.

And your story?

It's not over.

But what you've lived so far is more valuable than you know.

So share it—not to impress, but to invest in others.

Living Legacy Is a Daily Practice

Legacy doesn't begin when your life is summarized.

It begins when your life is prioritized.

You don't need a eulogy to measure your impact.

You can feel it now—in the ripple effect of your daily actions.

Every time you:

- Live out your values with clarity
- Speak truth with gentleness
- Encourage instead of criticize
- Serve instead of wait
- Show up instead of shut down

You are living your legacy.

Legacy is not someday.
It's now.

It's how you hold space for a hurting friend.

It's how you stay curious when the world gets loud.

It's how you keep your heart open, even when life's been hard.

And maybe, most importantly—it's how you choose to be present.

Because presence is the most unforgettable gift you can give.

And presence is what legacy is made of.

So here's your invitation:

Don't just leave a legacy.
Live one.

Right now. Right where you are.

One intentional moment at a time.

Conclusion
Living Forward with Intention

If you've made it to this page, I want to say thank you—

Not just for reading, but for traveling with me.

For allowing this book to be more than paper and ink—

For letting it be a conversation. A mirror. A map.

We've walked through the practical, the emotional, and the spiritual terrain of retirement together.

We've explored what it means to create a second act that's not just tolerable—but truly alive.

And now, we arrive at this moment—not with a list of final answers, but with better questions.

- Who am I now, without the titles I used to wear?
- What does a meaningful day look like, now that I get to choose?
- What do I still have to give—and what beauty might I be ready to receive?

These are not quick questions. They're not one-time journal prompts.

They are living questions—the kind you return to, again and again, like the sunrise.

And here's the beautiful truth:

There is no one right way to retire.
There is only your way.
Your rhythm.
Your voice.
Your joy.
Your evolving truth.

And the more permission you give yourself to define this time on your terms,

The more this season will become not just meaningful—but magical.

This Isn't the End—It's a Beginning

You're not retiring from life.

You're stepping more fully into it.

Into the parts you used to rush through.

Into the conversations you used to postpone.

Into the creativity, the rest, the connection that may have waited decades for your attention.

You now have time, space, and freedom—
Not just to do, but to be.

And that is a rare and sacred invitation.

Whether you spend your days taking long walks, writing your memoir, babysitting grandkids, mentoring a new generation, or simply savoring slow mornings—

You are shaping a life with meaning.
A life that reflects you.

Not who you were expected to be.

But who you've always wanted to become.

Let This Be Your Declaration

Let this book be more than content.

Let it be your catalyst.

To pause.

To listen inward.

To imagine again.

To dream with both feet on the ground.

Maybe this is the chapter where you finally:
- Start that book
- Learn to paint
- Take that trip
- Host that dinner
- Join that class
- Rebuild that friendship
- Forgive yourself for something old
- Or say yes to something entirely new

Whatever it is—large or quiet—you deserve it.

Not because you earned it, but because life is a gift, and you are still here to live it.

You're not done.

You're just beginning again—more grounded, more present, more awake.

I'm With You

This isn't just a book I wrote.

It's a path I'm walking, too.

I'm figuring it out—just like you.

Still asking questions. Still making adjustments.

Still learning how to live on purpose—without all the old roles, schedules, or expectations.

But one thing I know for sure?

The journey is always richer when it's shared.

So wherever your path takes you from here,

Know this:

You're not alone.
You are part of something bigger.
And your second act? It might just be the truest one yet.

Let's keep walking together—

With clarity, with courage, and yes, with a little fun along the way.

To your second act,

Gary

Embracing Retirement Workbook

Reflection Questions to Accompany Each Chapter

Welcome to the Embracing Retirement Workbook

This isn't just a set of questions.

It's a space for reflection, reconnection, and renewal.

Whether you're newly retired or years into this chapter, taking time to reflect is one of the most powerful ways to live on purpose. This workbook is your guide—not to tell you what to do, but to help you listen inward and respond with clarity.

You don't have to answer every question. You don't have to go in order. You don't even have to write anything down (though we hope you do).

The only requirement? Be honest with yourself.

Because your life is still unfolding. And these pages are here to help you shape it intentionally, lovingly, and with joy.

The Question That Changes Everything

- What do I want retirement to feel like—not just look like on paper?

- What emotions do I want to experience more frequently in this season of life?

- Who am I becoming, now that I'm no longer defined by my previous roles or titles?

Designing Your Days with Intention

- What are three activities that consistently give me energy and joy?

- If I could create a meaningful morning routine, what would it include?

- How can I structure my week to reflect what I value most?

Reconnecting with Purpose

- When do I feel most needed, energized, or alive?

- What parts of my past work or identity do I miss—and why?

- What kind of impact do I still feel called to make in the world around me?

The Power of Contribution

- What talents, experiences, or wisdom do I still want to share?

- Where do I feel naturally drawn to serve, mentor, or support others?

- What small act of kindness or contribution could I offer someone this week?

The Emotional Undercurrents

- What feelings have surfaced in me during this retirement transition—expected or unexpected?

- What parts of my former life do I need to grieve or honor before I can move forward?

- What version of myself is beginning to emerge in this new chapter?

Relationships in Transition

- Which of my current relationships feel most nourishing and life-giving?

- Are there relationships that need healing, redefining, or releasing?

- What does meaningful connection look like to me now—and who do I want to share it with?

<u>Staying Sharp—Mind, Body, and Spirit</u>

- What helps me feel vibrant—mentally, physically, and emotionally?

- What small daily or weekly habit would help me feel more alive?

- How am I tending to my mind, body, and spirit as forms of self-respect and care?

Planning for the Unexpected

- What potential challenges am I most concerned about—and how can I gently prepare for them?

- Who are the trusted people in my life who can support me through transitions or crises?

- What practical steps (legal, medical, financial, emotional) can I take now to reduce stress later?

Reimagining Work in Retirement

- What type of work—or contribution—still brings me a sense of joy or purpose?

- Is there a skill, passion, or idea I've been longing to explore or share?

- What would "working" look like if I got to define it entirely on my own terms?

Creativity in the Second Act

- What creative spark have I set aside that I might now reclaim?

- How can I create space in my life for creative expression—no matter how small?

- When was the last time I felt playful, curious, or expressive—and how can I feel that more often?

A Retirement Built on Gratitude

- What are three small things I'm grateful for today?

- How does gratitude shift the way I see myself and the world around me?

- How might I live gratitude—not just feel it—as part of my daily rhythm and legacy?

Living Your Legacy

"Carve your name on hearts, not tombstones. A legacy is etched into the minds of others and the stories they share about you." – Shannon L. Alder

Part 1:

Reflection – What Legacy Means to You

1. When you hear the word "legacy," what emotions or thoughts come to mind?

(Write freely—this is your definition, not a dictionary's.)

2. Legacy is not just what you leave behind, but what you live out daily.

What values do you want to embody in this chapter of life?

☐ Kindness

☐ Courage

☐ Generosity

☐ Wisdom

☐ Creativity

☐ Faith

☐ Service

☐ Joy

☐ [Other: _____]

Choose your top 3 values.

Write a sentence about how you can actively live each one today:

- Value 1:
- Value 2:
- Value 3:

Part 2:
Your Ripple Effect

3. Who are three people you've positively influenced—knowingly or unknowingly?

Reflect on how you've impacted them.

- Name:

    Impact I had:

- Name:

    Impact I had:

- Name:

    Impact I had:

Now flip it—who's left a legacy in you? What can you learn from their example?

Part 3:
Intentional Acts of Legacy

Legacy doesn't require wealth or a monument—it often shows up in small, consistent actions.

4. What legacy-building action can you take this month? Choose one or more:

☐ Write a letter to your children or grandchildren

☐ Mentor someone starting out in your former field

☐ Share a personal story that teaches a life lesson

☐ Make a charitable donation aligned with your values

☐ Start a creative project you've always dreamed of

☐ Record a video message for future generations

☐ [Your own idea: _____]

What will you do in the next 7 days to begin?

(Be specific: what, when, and how?)

Part 4:

Your Legacy Statement

5. Write your "living legacy" statement in 2–3 sentences.

This isn't about how you want to be remembered after you're gone—it's about how you want to live right now.

"I want to live my life in a way that…"
(You fill in the rest.)

How to Use This Workbook Moving Forward

- Use it as a journaling tool—one question at a time, one day at a time.
- Return to it yearly to revisit how your answers evolve.
- Reflect with a partner, a small group, or a trusted coach or mentor.
- Highlight questions that stir something in you.
- Celebrate your own growth by tracking meaningful shifts and new insights.

You don't need perfect answers. You don't need a plan for everything.

You just need a willingness to pause, reflect, and move forward with intention.

Your second act is yours to shape.

This workbook is simply here to remind you that the answers are already within you.

About the Author

Gary Fretwell is a #1 International Bestselling Author of The Magic of a Moment; a book celebrated for its heart-centered wisdom and inspiring reflections on the power of everyday choices. With decades of experience in higher education and leadership consulting, Gary has worked with nearly 1,000 institutions across North America, guiding individuals and organizations through meaningful transformation.

Known for his warm, insightful approach, Gary is also the author of Unlocking the Magic Daily Journal, a practical companion designed to help readers turn inspiration into daily action.

In his newest work, Embracing Retirement: Discovering Your Fulfilling Second Act, Gary invites readers to reimagine this life chapter with purpose, passion, and joy. His message is clear: retirement isn't an end—it's a new beginning.

When he's not writing or speaking, Gary serves as President of Prescott Meals on Wheels and enjoys spending time with his wife Nancy and their golden retrievers. Whether on the page or in person, Gary's mission remains the same: to encourage others to live fully, act boldly, and make each moment count.

Website: https://garyfretwell.com

Email: fretwgl@gmail.com

LinkedIn: https://www.linkedin.com/in/gary-fretwell-36691b6/

Facebook: https://www.facebook.com/gfretwell

X: @fretwgl

Enjoyed the Book? Help Others Discover It.

If *Embracing Retirement* resonated with you, I'd be so grateful if you'd take just a moment to leave a quick star rating on Amazon.

You may have seen a pop-up rating on your Kindle when you finished reading—but this is a different one that stays visible to future readers.

Even if you don't write a full review, just clicking on a star makes a big difference. It helps others decide if this book is right for them—and it helps me continue writing books that matter.

If you do have a few extra seconds to share a sentence or two, I'd love to hear what stood out to you.

Thanks so much for being part of this journey. I hope to see you again in the next book.

Warmly,

Gary

Made in the USA
Columbia, SC
11 June 2025